MOTHER
TERESA

FRIEND OF THE POOR

by Kathleen Kudlinski

Aladdin Paperbacks
New York London Toronto Sydney

For Doe Boyle, whose faith inspires me

With special thanks to Nancy Hough,
Volunteer at Our Lady of Grace Monastery,
Dominican Nuns, Guilford, Connecticut

❧ ALADDIN PAPERBACKS
An imprint of Simon & Schuster Children's Publishing Division
1230 Avenue of the Americas, New York, NY 10020
Text copyright © 2006 by Kathleen Kudlinski
All rights reserved, including the right of reproduction
in whole or in part in any form.
ALADDIN PAPERBACKS and colophon
are trademarks of Simon & Schuster, Inc.
CHILDHOOD OF WORLD FIGURES
is registered trademark of Simon & Schuster, Inc.
Designed by Lisa Vega
The text of this book was set in Aldine 721.
Manufactured in the United States of America
First Aladdin Paperbacks edition February 2006
10 9 8 7 6 5 4 3 2 1
Library of Congress Control Number 2005929613
ISBN 13: 978-1-4169-1160-9
ISBN-10: 1-4169-1160-X

CONTENTS

CHAPTER ONE

FAMILY MEAL

"Gonxha Bojaxhiu!" the teacher called out.

"Yes, ma'am?" Gonxha smoothed her uniform as she rose to stand in the aisle beside her school desk.

"Lazar is here to take you home." Gonxha silently gathered her first-grade reader and her lunch pail and walked to the door. "I'll see you on Sunday." The teacher smiled. "Until then, God be with you."

Lazar took his sister's hand and led her out to the front steps of the Roman Catholic Church of the Sacred Heart, in Skopje, Macedonia.

"Why do I need a third grader to walk me home?" Gonxha asked her brother. "I'm big now, big enough to know it is 1917."

"Did you just learn that today, *'big girl'*?" Lazar laughed. His little sister was the tiniest girl in the first grade. Their teenage sister Agatha was taller, but she was already at home, working. The church bell chimed over their heads as they stepped onto the street. The deep gong of the Eastern Orthodox Church down the street chimed in. Then an imam's voice soared from the nearest minaret calling Muslims to prayer.

Gonxha spread her arms and danced a circle on the cobblestones, letting all the joyful noises fill her heart. Three old women stopped to clap time for her and call out in Serbian. Gonxha didn't understand their language, but she could read the smiles on their tired faces. A Turkish woman stopped in the doorway of her spice shop and nodded happily at her.

"Stop it, Gonxha! You can't dance in the street," Lazar said, and pulled her out of the way of a donkey cart loaded with beets and carrots.

The farmer waved at Gonxha. "Dance on,

little one," he said in Albanian. "Skopje needs more sunshine like you."

"See?" Gonxha felt an angry flush rise to her cheeks. "You are wrong, Lazar! People like it when I dance. They like it when I sing, too." She began to sing the song Papa had taught her.

"Stop it!" Lazar put a hand over Gonxha's mouth. He pulled her into an alley. "You could get attacked in Skopje for singing that song." He let Gonxha go and smoothed her hair. "Before you were born, there was a war here. Albania broke away to become its own country."

"But we aren't in Albania," Gonxha said, confused.

"No." Lazar took her hand again and they headed for home. "When they made the borders, our town was left in Macedonia. But people are still mad about the war."

"Mad enough to hurt me?" Gonxha felt tears rise in her eyes. Lazar stopped and hugged his sister. "Not here," he said. "It mostly happens more in other cities near the border."

"Where Papa goes for *meetings*?" Gonxha felt chilled with fear.

"Oh, Gonxha!" Lazar slapped his forehead. "I forgot. Mama said to hurry. Papa is coming home from a trip to Turkey tonight! He should have new rugs to sell. People will want them in the houses he builds. "Together they ran down the hill to their home on Vlaska Street, one of the biggest houses on the block.

Lazar took the front stairs two at a time and rushed in. "Mama! Mama!" he called.

"Wait, Lazar, wait!" Gonxha shouted. She stood until he returned to the doorway, then she pointed at the cup of holy water attached to the door frame. "You forgot. We are Roman Catholic. There's things we must do."

Lazar rolled his eyes and sighed. Gonxha waited. She watched her brother dip his fingers into the holy water and cross himself, then she blessed herself, too, touching forehead and heart, then left shoulder and right. "In the name of the Father and the Son," she said clearly, "and the Holy Ghost. Amen. Lazar," she said, without a break, "I could not forget this. My first Communion is this weekend."

"I know, I know," Lazar said. "It is all you have talked about for weeks."

"Children," Mama said, stepping out of the kitchen, "get out of your school clothes at once. Gonxha, I need grape leaves for dinner tonight. Lazar, I have a basket of food for you to take to the poor family down the street."

"But those people aren't in our church."

"For shame, Lazar." Mama's voice sounded sharp as a knife, then softened as she quoted from the Bible, "Whatsoever you do unto the least of these, my brethren, you do unto me."

Gonxha remembered how her mother sent basket after basket to hungry or sick neighbors. Suddenly it made sense. "It is like we are feeding a hungry Jesus?" she asked.

Mama nodded. "My Little Flower," she said, softly. Gonxha loved having a name that meant something so pretty in Albanian.

"I'll take the food now," Lazar said, and slunk out with a basket laden with rice and mint-scented meatballs in yogurt sauce.

Gonxha hung her uniform and petticoat in the clothes press in her room and changed into a house dress. Outside, she stood on tiptoe in the back courtyard to reach the largest new leaves in the grape arbor, then hurried back into the kitchen. It was full of steam and scented with lemon and spicy sausage.

"Bring those leaves here," Agatha said. Gonxha stepped beside her older sister and, one by one, handed her the leaves. Agatha dipped them into the boiling water, then turned to spread them on a board.

Mama scooped spoonfuls of fried sausage and rice from her skillet into the center of each leaf. She wrapped the edges of the leaves around the stuffing then rolled them over, making tidy little loaves. Agatha set them into another pot. "I'll squeeze lemons for the sauce," Mama said. "Agatha, get a crock of yogurt from the cellar. Gonxha, bring up a scuttle of coal. The stove has to be hotter to bake the cookies."

Gonxha's mouth watered thinking of the honey-soaked cookies that would follow this special dinner. *For me*, she thought. *My first Communion.* She shivered with the thought of it. A party dinner. Her first confession. And then Communion, itself. Even her teacher was coming to watch! Gonxha said a silent prayer that she would do everything right.

Later, when Agatha had tied Gonxha's hair in bows and Mama had checked behind Lazar's ears for dirt, after the oil lamps were lit and the table set, Mama put on her best dress. Then they waited. The china clock ticked loudly in the front hall. "Get your mandolin, Agatha," Mama said, her voice tense. "We can sing while we wait for your papa to get home."

"Hello!" They all jumped as the front door squeaked open.

"Papa!" Lazar leaped to get his father's coat. Mr. Bojaxhiu took the stiff felt fez off his head and gave it to Agatha to hang on the coatrack.

He smoothed his wavy black hair back down and stroked his broad mustache.

Mama patted his arm. "Haven't you forgotten something?" she asked, and glanced at Gonxha. "Oh, yes," Papa said. "Some of my freedom-fighting friends will be coming in tonight. Would you sing for us, Little Flower—and you, too, Agatha?"

"Albania forever!" Lazar shouted.

"Nikola," Mama said coldly. "This is the night to celebrate Gonxha's first confession. The children don't need to be part of your political meetings."

"We're all part of it, Drana." Papa sounded tired. "It is 1915. We should have had independence long ago, but the violence is spreading. We will get a free Albania yet!"

"There will be no guns in here," Mama warned. "Not with the children."

Papa did not answer, but Gonxha squirmed with excitement. Now there would be secret guests at her special dinner. Perhaps Papa would ask her to dress up to sing and dance with Agatha! That was always fun. And late into the night, she could lie in bed listening to Papa's important voice booming while the others listened and took orders. It was the best lullaby she could imagine.

"Do not let your politics make you forget about Gonxha's first Communion on Sunday," Mama scolded.

Papa reached down and patted Gonxha's head. "My big girl," he said. Gonxha grinned at Lazar. Papa bowed his head and said an extra-long grace over the food. Before everyone said amen and crossed themselves, Gonxha heard Papa pray, "May God welcome this little flower to the front of our church." She sat straighter. After Sunday, life would change. When she went to church with her mother every morning, she could line up with all the grown-ups at the altar rail instead of sit alone in the pew.

After the blessing at the end of the meal, Mama shooed them out of the dining room. "I will put on fresh coffee while the children dress, Nikola. Lazar, gather the oil lamps into the parlor, cut back their wicks, and wipe any extra soot from their chimneys. There is extra coal oil in the jug by the back steps."

Gonxha ran upstairs and pulled her house dress off. Agatha opened the great wooden chest and took out the knee-length blouses, stiff with black and red embroidery. Gonxha hummed as she put hers on. She tied the strings to the red apron, thick as a carpet with embroidery. "Take your time," Agatha said. "Papa will expect your costume to be perfect. His grandmother stitched every one of those patterns with her own hands, you know." Gonxha stared at herself in the mirror in the traditional Albanian costume. Her cheeks were pink, her eyes were brown, and her hair was dark and wavy where it disappeared under the big linen kerchief. She spun a circle in delight.

"Look down," Agatha reminded her.

"Oh, I forgot shoes!" Gonxha wiggled her toes.

Agatha laughed and handed her baggy woolen trousers. "These first, silly girl," she teased. Then she helped Gonxha curl the points of her shoes upward. "There," she said finally.

"These clothes are so hot," Gonxha said. "And they are heavy."

"Could you imagine wearing them all the time? Our people used to," Agatha said. "Some of the old ladies still do." She took a last look at her sister and smiled. "Are we ready?"

Downstairs, a dozen men had gathered in the parlor. Mama hurried in and out, serving thick, black coffee. The licorice scent of ouzo, a liqueur, hung in the air with the aroma of sweat. *Freedom fighters*, Gonxha thought. She stared at them, wondering if any had guns. Agatha strummed her mandolin and then tuned its strings. She had to nudge Gonxha to make her start singing. At the first words to Papa's favorite Albanian folk tune, half the men rose to their feet. By the end, they were all standing, their glasses raised. The last tune

Agatha played was a hymn. She sang the melody, and Gonxha's high, sweet voice wove its own pattern above and below, in perfect harmony.

"They are nightingales!" one man said.

"Angels," another cheered.

A third wiped his eyes with a big handkerchief.

Papa beamed.

After one last baklava cookie drenched in honey and nuts, and a pat on the head from Papa, Agatha and Gonxha headed up to bed. Agatha carefully folded their precious costumes while Gonxha pulled on a long nightgown and a nightcap. She stared across the room at the first Communion dress that was hanging ready for Sunday morning. It was so very white compared with the cherry red and colorful stitching of Albanian dress! Sometimes Gonxha wore a white kerchief over her hair, and sometimes a white blouse, but never had she worn so much pure white. It made her feel squirmy inside to think what it meant.

Her heart wasn't pure enough yet to receive Communion. First she had to go to confession.

On Saturday morning, Gonxha waited with her mother in a pew in the dim light of the church. She looked at the stained-glass windows and thought about what sins she would confess to the priest. There were no mortal sins she could think of, where she had known something was really, really bad but she had done it, anyway. The thought of doing something so awful made her stomach feel sick. But *venial* sins—little sins when she forgot to be good? She had done those. Not helping a classmate with her reading. Being impatient with her brother. Being overly proud of her family. Gonxha reached for her mother's hand.

Can I actually say them aloud? she wondered. *What if my penalty is too hard?* Tears came to her eyes at the thought. What if she could never be forgiven?

Mrs. Bojaxhiu nudged Gonxha and pointed

toward an open door. Gonxha dragged herself into the confession booth. It was like a dark little closet, with a kneeling bench inside. She took a deep breath, closed the door, and knelt on the cushion. It was quiet in there, and scented with sweet incense. In the darkness she felt peaceful and somehow close to God.

Just as Gonxha folded her hands and bowed her head to pray, *snap!* another little door opened. A priest on the other side whispered, "Yes, my child?"

"Forgive me, Father," Gonxha said as she had been told, "for I have sinned." It was surprisingly easy to whisper her sins into the warm darkness. She even confessed a few she hadn't realized were bothering her. When she couldn't think of any more, she whispered an apology and promised to do better.

Then the priest forgave her in Christ's name and whispered, "You must say four Our Father prayers and apologize to your brother."

Gonxha felt weak with relief. Those were things she could do! Then her sins would be erased forever and her heart would be pure again. Her breathing came quick and shallow. "Pray with me," the priest murmured. Gonxha had practiced the Latin words to the Act of Contrition so her voice and the priest's blended together. Then the priest blessed her and Snap! his little door shut again.

It was over! Suddenly Gonxha felt she could fly. She opened the door and squinted into the bright light of the church. Her mother waved from the pew. Gonxha tried to walk in a dignified way, but instead she skipped down the aisle. She dropped to her knees on the soft cushion, just like the gown-ups did. She blessed herself and made a steeple with her fingers, then closed her eyes tight. Gonxha thought every single word as she said it: "Our Father who art in heaven . . ." It sounded different the second time, and by the fourth time, the old prayer seemed to have a whole new meaning.

Gonxha turned to face her mother and smiled. Now when she walked, she did not need to skip. She felt clean. Pure. On her way out of the church, Gonxha stopped to dip her fingers into holy water and bless herself. "I have something to say to Lazar," she told her mother, then led the way down the street walking tall.

"Lazar," she said. "I am sorry I yelled at you in the street. And again by the front door."

Lazar scratched his head. "You yelled? When?" They both laughed, and Gonxha felt a sudden rush of love for her brother.

As the day went on, things seemed more and more normal. A neighbor came by to play, and Mama had chores that needed to be done. At the dinner table, Gonxha sat up and ate like a lady. *I am pure*, she thought. She looked around. Everyone in her family went to confession every week. They all had felt this floating feeling. It was like a secret they all shared. "I'm glad we go to Sacred Heart," she said.

"Just wait until tomorrow!" Agatha said.

On Sunday, Gonxha watched closely as the priest spoke the ancient Latin words that ceremoniously changed wine into Christ's blood and a thin Eucharist wafer into His body. She shivered with excitement as the bells jingled during the transformation. She felt dizzy with the smell of incense. Gonxha was almost dreamwalking when she made her way to the little fence around the altar. She knelt with the other first graders and folded her hands on the altar rail. When the priest approached her, she looked up at his face. Then Gonxha opened her mouth and waited.

She felt the blessed Sacrament of the Eucharist land on her tongue. Her mouth shut with surprise. It was real. It was in her mouth. And it was dissolving, becoming part of her.

She turned calmly to walk back to sit with her family. A wonderful new feeling warmed her like a hug. She was not alone. Every member of the church, living or dead, stretching all the way back to Christ and his friends, had done the very same ceremony. This morning, Roman Catholics all around the world heard the same Latin words, too, and tasted the same blessed Sacrament.

Suddenly Gonxha wanted to twirl and dance, skip and sing. Instead, she slid into her family's pew and squeezed her mother's hand as tightly as she could.

CHAPTER TWO

POISON

"Where is Papa tonight?" Gonxha asked. "Is he in Italy again? Or Egypt this time?" She thought about the globe in her third-grade classroom.

"Will he and Mr. Morten bring their wagon load of fancy fabrics home soon? I love to see them all before they go to the shop."

"You just love the gifts Papa brings you when he travels," Lazar said, pulling the point on Gonxha's head scarf.

"Lazar!" Mama scolded. She set down the basket of food she was carrying and helped cover her daughter's hair again. "Your papa is in Belgrade at another political meeting." Her voice trembled, and Gonxha looked up at her face. There was fear in her eyes. "Morten stayed home. He has no taste for danger," Mama said. "He makes a good business partner for your papa."

Gonxha took her mother's hand in her own. "Mama, I pray for Papa every morning in church after Mass."

"I do too," Mama whispered. Together, the Bojaxhius headed down the street to visit a sick neighbor. At the corner house, Lazar knocked at the door. "Alzet?" Mama called. There was no answer, but Mama led them in. "Light a candle, Agatha. Get some coal and heat up the stove, Lazar. It is so cold in here!" Gonxha followed her mother into the bedroom, where a woman lay sunken under stained covers. Gonxha's nose twitched at the smell.

"Is that you, Drana? Thank God." The old woman's skeletal hand trembled as it reached toward Mrs. Bojaxhiu. "And your Little Flower? That tiny one is such a blessing."

Gonxha reached down and slid Alzet's smelly bedpan out from under the bed. She carried it to the outhouse, emptied it, and picked a flower on the way back indoors. Agatha was stirring a pot of broth on top of the stove. "She is worse," Gonxha told her. "Lazar, you could sweep this floor."

She ducked as her brother tried to grab her head scarf again. Back in the bedroom, Mama sat on the side of the bed, brushing the woman's stringy hair from her forehead. Gonxha returned the bedpan and stuck the flower into a glass. "Get some water, Gonxha," Mama said quietly. "And a cloth." Gonxha hurried back out to the kitchen and pumped a bowl of water. Then she grabbed a tattered towel.

"You're going to *touch* her?" Lazar said, shaking his head. As Gonxha left the kitchen she heard Lazar tell Agatha, "Our Little Flower is almost as good as Mama." Gonxha was smiling when she entered the bedroom.

"A smile like that brightens the world," Mama said. She eased off the bed. "If you will wipe Alzet's face before she eats, I will straighten her bedclothes." Gonxha swallowed as she dipped the towel in water, then patted the old woman's scabby face. "Where is that smile?" Mama prompted.

Gonxha made herself smile. Slowly, Alzet smiled back. Gonxha could see how pretty she must have once been. "Soup!" Agatha announced, carrying it in. Mama spoon-fed the old woman. Before the bowl was half emptied, Alzet fell asleep again. As Mama pulled the covers up to her chin, Gonxha stared at the woman's face. The prettiness was gone again, lost in a wince of pain, sunken cheeks, and wrinkled skin.

"She cannot live alone much longer," Mama said as the children cleaned up. No one answered. They knew Alzet would be moving into their house until she was better—or until she died. Mama and the children gathered around Alzet's bed and prayed before they left.

"I'm hungry," Lazar said when they were out on the street again.

"Always," Mama said. "You eat like a billy goat, Lazar—anything, anytime. You will be as tall as your father before long." Gonxha coughed with the exertion of keeping up with her long-legged family. "You, my little one," Mama said. "You eat like a sparrow. A little peck here, a little peck there. No wonder you are still bird-size!"

"'Gluttony is a sin,'" Gonxha quoted her Sunday school teacher. "'There are so many hungry people in the world. . . .'"

"What is that?" Lazar asked as they rounded the corner. "A wagon by our door? Papa is home?"

They rushed to the house and in through the open door. "Nikola?" Mama called.

"In here, Mrs. Bojaxhiu," a strange man's voice called from the bedroom. Gonxha carefully closed the door and blessed herself with holy water before going in. Papa lay on the bed, groaning. He grabbed at his stomach and mumbled words that made no sense. Worst of all, when he turned his head toward Gonxha, his eyes did not find her.

"Out," Mama said, and shooed them away. Agatha put her arm around Gonxha and herded her back toward the kitchen.

"What is wrong with Papa?" Gonxha was trembling all over.

"Maybe something he ate at his meeting?" Lazar guessed. "Agatha, could you put dinner together? Mama will be hungry soon." The three children sat looking at flatbread and yogurt and grapes. Not even Lazar ate, though Papa's friend grabbed a handful of grapes as he left.

At the sound of Papa throwing up, Lazar jumped to his feet. "Now he'll be fine," he said. Mama made a frightened little shriek, and Gonxha froze. Agatha and Lazar ran to the bedroom, but Gonxha could not move. She sat stiff, praying as hard as she could.

"Little Flower!" Gonxha looked up. Mama stood at the door. Her face was pale, and the front of her dress was spattered with blood. "Get a priest," she said. "Now." Then Mama was gone, back to the bedroom.

Gonxha crossed herself and rose slowly. She blessed herself again at the door. *A priest?* she thought. *Is Papa dying?* Her mind stopped working, but her feet hurried her to the church. The priest was not in. Something told her to head toward the railroad station. *Find a priest.* Mama trusted her. She would not let Mama down.

There! Under the streetlamp, in the long, black skirts of a cassock. It was a priest. "Father!" she called. "Come quick. My papa . . ."

The priest followed her home and rushed into the bedroom. Gonxha waited in the hall. She heard her mother's sobs of relief. Then she heard the priest's soothing voice begin repeating Psalm 51 from the Bible. Then he prayed to God and to the angels to help Papa. Lazar and Agatha silently wandered out to the hallway.

Mama came, too, just as silent, but with tears streaming down her face and a Rosary clutched in her hands. Gonxha sat down with them at the table, not wanting to think of Papa saying his last confession. And she definitely did *not* want to think of the priest making the sign of the cross on Papa's forehead with holy oil.

It was very late that night before the priest left the room to get Mama. "He still lives," he said gently.

"Go to bed," Mama said, looking at her children. "Pray."

The next day, Gonxha's father died at the hospital. Friends brought food to the house and held Mama while she cried. Lazar stood in the backyard, pulling at the grapevines. Agatha sat with her teenage classmates. Gonxha did not know what to do. She wandered from room to room, listening now and then to what the grown-ups were saying.

"Such a good man," said one of the aunts, who had gathered into a little knot. Two of them sobbed aloud. "A good provider," another one said.

"Rich," one of them said, fingering a linen tablecloth.

"But look how much he gave to the church!"

"And to the poor." More tears.

"He was so brave in the war," his business partner said.

"Too brave. Too political." Gonxha recognized one of the freedom fighters. His voice became quiet, and she leaned closer to hear. "Seems to me like Nikola was poisoned."

One of the men glanced at Gonxha. "The girl!" he whispered. "Shhh." They all stepped back, coughing or gulping coffee, or looking at their fingernails.

Poisoned. Gonxha tucked that thought away to consider later—when she could think straight. For now, life was a strange blur. No one was acting normal. And the house was full—so full—of so many people. Who would have thought her father had so many friends?

At last the priest gathered them all to say the Rosary together. Gonxha still had hers from her first Communion. She padded upstairs to get it and forgot what she was looking for. "Gonxha!" Agatha called up from the front hall. Gonxha jumped, grabbed her Rosary, and hurried downstairs. The bottom stair was the only place left to sit, so she and Agatha squeezed in together.

The girls' elbows knocked together as they each found the crucifix dangling at the end of their sets of beads. Gonxha looked around the room crowded with visitors. It stunk of bodies and food and cigarettes. *There is no air*, Gonxha thought. For a minute, she felt sick, and then everyone in the room was blessing themselves. Gonxha's fingers moved along the Rosary automatically. Her mouth made the right words too. First, as she held the crucifix, she recited the Apostles Creed. It was done before Gonxha realized it. Next, she felt the biggest bead—the Our Father prayer. Everyone said it. Then she felt for three small beads. "Hail Mary, full of grace." The room filled with hushed, calm voices speaking together, breathing together.

Gonxha felt herself relax. Bead after bead slipped through her fingers, each full of meaning.

The Rosary was about Mary, mother of God,

pure, sweet, holy Mary—but that wasn't all. While Gonxha murmured a prayer with each bead, she had to keep track of which mystery to think about. Her lips moved on as her mind imagined, first, the joyful mysteries of Jesus' life. Then the sorrowful ones as he was killed. Then finally the glorious mysteries of the end of His life.

Saying the Rosary took all of her attention. It was like being in a cocoon where nothing could hurt her. Gonxha wanted it never to end.

The final prayer was Hail Holy Queen. Then the room was quiet. Faces looked relaxed. No one was crying.

Gonxha carried the Rosary in her pocket for the next few days. She stuck her hand in and felt it when she needed strength during the funeral. She recited the prayers whenever she needed comfort. It made her feel calm. Papa might be gone, but Mary and Jesus were as close as her pocket.

★ ★ ★

It almost seemed that Mama was gone too. She sat and sighed instead of cooked. She cried. She did not want to walk to church for morning Mass—and then she did not want to leave church when it was over.

Agatha took over the shopping and cooking. Lazar worked in the yard and hauled coal. Gonxha washed and swept and tried to keep the clothes clean. Sometimes Mama helped. Other times she just went to bed.

"Mama!" Gonxha called one morning. "Morten is here to see you!" Papa's business partner strolled into the front hall and looked around. Suddenly Gonxha could see dust in the corner. The windows needed washing too.

"Drana!" he said as Mama wandered in from her room. "How are you, dear?"

Mama's eyes filled with tears again. "She is fine," Gonxha said quickly. Mama settled into the nearest chair.

Agatha came in from the kitchen. "It is good to see you, Morten," she said. "We need to talk about money. I'm almost out." Gonxha stared at her sister. Agatha had been running the household by herself.

"Well," Morten said. He shifted his feet. "I'm not comfortable speaking of this." He smoothed down his big mustache. The movement reminded Gonxha of Papa. That was what the men did. They grew mustaches, made money, and managed the house.

Unless they died.

Gonxha stared at Agatha. Her sister seemed to be growing taller right there in the hallway. "Morten," she said, "we must have some of Papa's money."

"Well, to be perfectly honest"—Morten rubbed his nose—"business hasn't been the same since he, er, left. There aren't any extra funds. In fact, I was here to ask you to repay a loan I made to your father a few years back. . . ."

"Nikola never loaned you a drachma!" Agatha and Gonxha whipped around to stare at their mother. She was standing. She was speaking.

She stalked toward Morten. "How *dare* you?" she spat.

Morten took a step backward. "I did not mean to upset you," he said. "But I really must insist—"

"You may leave," Mama said. "*Now.* My cousin, the lawyer, will contact you."

As the door closed behind Morten, Gonxha clapped her hands. "That was wonderful, Mama!" Agatha cried.

"I have to lie down," Mama said. She seemed to shrink as she shuffled back to her bedroom. At the end of the afternoon, though, Mama was back. She shooed Agatha out of the kitchen. She complained about the dust and the sorry state of the grapevines. She made dinner and then she led the blessing.

"What do we do now?" Agatha asked as everyone dug into the lamb and walnuts.

"I will open my own business," Mama said firmly.

"But you are a mother!" Gonxha gasped. "*My* mother!" She thought fast. No mother she knew ran a business. Not in Skopje. Not in 1919.

"How can you do this without a man?" Lazar said.

"I will need your help." Mama was looking straight at Gonxha. "I will need all of your help. I know fabric. I know fine needlework. We may have lost Morten," she said the name as if it were a disease, "but our old customers know the good Bojaxhiu name."

"What will we do for money to start?" Agatha challenged.

It seemed that Mama had thought it all through. They sold some of their furniture and fine old tablecloths. They sold silverware, too. They sold the clocks off their walls and the books off their shelves. But Mama used the money to make smart buys of specialty fabrics. She sold the goods at a profit, too, and bought more stock. Soon she needed a store—and she could afford to rent one herself.

Gonxha watched in amazement as her mother—a woman—started a business and then made it grow. She handled the finances. She made deals with astonished men. And, somehow, Mama still had the energy to help their needy neighbors. Alzet came to stay for a while until she died, peacefully, in the parlor. Mama invited hungry orphans to dinner and gave generously to the church. Mama walked Agatha, Lazar, and Gonxha to Mass every morning, too.

Gonxha walked to school alone now. This was her last year in the Albanian-speaking church school. For fourth grade at her new school, she'd have to speak the Serbo-Croat language. Lazar told her it was easy to pick up, so she wasn't worried. She had the Rosary in her pocket, Communion every morning, and confession every weekend.

When the teacher told the class that many people around the globe did not belong to the Church, she felt bad for them. They did not know how safe and happy they could be! "Our people go to these far off places," the teacher said, "as nurses or teachers. While they are there, they bring our religion to people who have never heard about it." She spun the globe. "Missionaries help people here . . . and here . . . and here. . . ." As she paused, students called out the places his finger had landed.

"India!"

"South America!"

"Africa!" Gonxha imagined lions and zebras and a classroom full of little children. She thought about teaching children how to read and to write, to sing and to pray. She sat up straight in her seat. She could do that!

"In fact," the teacher said, "there is a letter here"—she opened a magazine—"from a missionary in Africa. Would anyone like to hear it?"

"Yes, m'am!" Gonxha's voice was so loud, everyone laughed. "Excuse me." She apologized, knowing she would have to do penance for this rudeness. The teacher laughed and then read the whole letter. When she was done, she left the magazine on Gonxha's desk.

"You may take it home tonight," she said.

"Bring it to me in church on Sunday. I'll lend you the back issues, too, if you want. Other mission letters come to the school library." Gonxha just nodded. She was already reading the letter again.

Outside of school, the Bojaxhiu family spent all their time together, going to church meetings in the evenings and working at the church on weekends. Agatha and Gonxha sang in the church choir and joined church clubs. Gonxha carried the Rosary in her pocket everywhere. She wanted to be strong like her mother, but now she knew she did not have to stay in little old Skopje. There was a whole spinning globe of places out there where she could live.

There was Africa.

CHAPTER THREE
CLIMBING
THE MOUNTAIN

"Mama, I'm twelve. Why can't I go with my Sunday school class?" Gonxha stood by her mother's new desk in the parlor. Since she did not have religion classes in her new school, she went to weekend school at the church. She covered her mouth and coughed.

"That is why," Mama said briskly. "You have missed enough school this year already. Climbing all the way up the mountain? You are not well enough to keep up with the others." She looked back at the line of figures she had been adding.

"But we used to do it as a family, Mama. And I loved visiting the Letnice chapel and praying to Our Lady of Black Mountain. . . ." Gonxha stopped herself. She was breaking one of the Ten Commandments. Again. "Oh, forgive me, Mama." *Honor thy father and thy mother.* It was such a simple rule. Gonxha bit her lip in frustration.

Mama sighed and put her pencil down. "I would like to make the trip too," Mama said. "Perhaps I can take the time away from business this year." Gonxha held her breath. "We might be able to go after your Confirmation this spring. Would you like that?"

"Oh, Mama!" Gonxha hugged her mother.

The next day at school she tried to tell a friend about the trip up into the mountains. "Why would you want to go there?" Denajda asked. Gonxha thought for a minute that she had misunderstood the girl's language. Serbo-Croat was different, but so was the Latin they spoke in church and the French they were learning in class.

Then Gonxha remembered: Denajada was Muslim. She *was* different. *All God's children,* Gonxha heard her mother's voice in her mind. *They are all God's children.* But a Muslim like

Denajda couldn't understand how important this was to her. Gonxha felt pulled to the Letnice chapel, as if something awaited her at the top of the mountain.

"It means a lot to me," she said carefully. "The mountaintop is so beautiful. It is covered with wildflowers. And the air is so clear up there, I feel closer to God."

"Oh," Denajda said politely. She opened her mathematics book. "Did you have trouble with the homework last night?" Gonxha smiled. Math came easy to her. Schoolwork did. If you worked hard enough, she had decided, all of it seemed easy. The girls bent their heads together as Gonxha explained how to multiply fractions.

She was always teaching. It felt good to help the younger children in church learn their catechism lessons. It was fun to lead the little children's games on the lawn after church. When five orphan children came to stay in the house that winter, Gonxha helped them with table manners, Bible stories, and bedtime prayers.

She walked them to church in the morning too. Sacred Heart had changed. A new order of priests, the Jesuits, had taken over the church and the school. Jesuits were trained as teachers and had strong ideas about how children should be taught. The new priest, Father Zadrima, carried a stick to remind children how to behave. Lazar grew to fear it, though Gonxha loved the quiet order the priest brought to Sacred Heart.

"I think I might like to be a teacher," she told him one day. Later, when an assistant priest came to help out at the church, Father Zadrima called for Gonxha.

"I need your help," Father Zadrima said. "My new assistant cannot speak Albanian very well. Could you translate for him in catechism classes?" Gonxha smiled with delight. Now her free time was spent teaching—and learning. There were hundreds and hundreds of questions in the official catechism book. The answers were right there too. It was an easy way to learn about God, about life and death, about sin and about church ceremonies, and much, much more. The priests had written them down so everyone would know exactly what Jesus and His Apostles had said. The little children only had to memorize the answers given in the catechism book to know what God wanted.

To help them learn, Gonxha had to do more than memorize. She had to understand the questions and their answers, too, so she could explain them to a child. The new priest helped her study the faith. She helped him study the Albanian language.

By spring, Gonxha was ready for any question the visiting bishop might ask as she joined the church. Other twelve-year-olds worried about their Confirmation ceremony. Not Gonxha. She stood at the front of the church, dressed in her prettiest dress. When it was her turn to be confirmed, she listened carefully to the bishop's question. The answer leaped into her mind. In front of the whole church, she gave a perfect answer to the visiting bishop. She knew not to smile, for that would show pride.

The bishop made the sign of the cross on her forehead with holy oil, marking her as one of Christ's own. Next in the ceremony the bishop reached out and slapped her cheek. It was much harder than she'd expected. It stung! She felt her face redden. That slap was supposed to warn her that there were spiritual challenges ahead. But her answer had been perfect! She didn't deserve to be struck while all these people watched. She covered her cheek with her hand.

The bishop rested his hands on her head and said, "Be sealed with the gift of the Holy Spirit." Then he blessed her and prayed over the Confirmation class and their godparents. The ceremony went on in Latin, welcoming the children into the church as soldiers of Christ. There was a party at church and a feast at home, but Gonxha kept remembering the feel of that smack.

Faith is not like that, she told herself. Papa's death had been a slap in her mother's life, of course. But Jesus never left you. Not if you were true to Him and followed all the rules.

"Gonxha!" Agatha scolded. "Pay attention. This is *your* party. The aunties want us to sing!" Afterward, the women clapped and asked for more. Lazar handed Gonxha a present: a tiny Bible for her pocket. The men raised their glasses in memory of Nikola. More cookies. More coffee. Then, at last, the guests began to leave.

"Gonxha," Mama said as she finally closed the door, "do you remember Alana? She needs a bed here. Can we postpone our trip to the mountain until she is well again?"

"Certainly, Mama," Gonxha said quickly. She could almost feel Jesus smile.

"Hers is the saddest story," Mama rushed on. "Alana's children are grown, but they will not help her. They have homes and food to share. But will they? No. They are tired of taking her in. That is why we must care for her. Do you mind? It won't be for long."

"It will be fine, Mama," Gonxha said.

Mrs. Bojaxhiu stared at her daughter. "You already said yes, didn't you?" Gonxha nodded. "You didn't need all the explanation?" Gonxha shook her head no. "You have indeed grown up!" Mama hugged her and then laughed. "Except you haven't grown taller."

"Mama," Gonxha began to complain, but changed her tone mid-sentence. "We are all God's children, tall *or* short."

Finally Mama and Gonxha boarded the train toward Black Mountain. Lazar and Agatha stayed home to mind Mama's thriving business. "Isn't this nice?" Mama said as the countryside sped by, summer green beyond the windows.

Halfway up the mountain, the train stopped. "How are you feeling?" Mama asked.

Gonxha just nodded. She was afraid an answer would start the coughing again. If it did, Mama would make her go home.

"You'll let me know if you get tired?" Mama said as they began the long, slow walk up to the Letnice chapel.

Gonxha smiled and pulled her hand out of her pocket to show her mother the Rosary. Then she started another silent cycle of prayers and walked on. Groups passed them: teenagers, a couple with little children, a school class. Their happy, excited voices filled the air and then faded away as they hurried ahead. Gonxha didn't stop praying—or walking. Mama matched her pace.

Toward the top of the mountain, the trees were shorter. Just as Gonxha remembered, the air was clearer. Over her head the sky seemed endless. Wildflowers covered the ground. The people they saw walking away from the chapel seemed calm and quiet.

Gonxha dipped her fingers into the holy water as she entered the chapel and blessed herself. A candle was lit over the altar, so she knew there was blessed Sacrament there, awaiting the next Mass. Gonxha bent on one knee, bowing slightly toward the altar and its precious gifts. She glanced once at the statue of Mary of the Mountains and slipped into a pew.

Then she eased the padded kneeling bench out from under the bench in front of her. She knelt and closed her eyes. She felt the kneeler shift as her mother's weight settled beside her.

Gonxha had many things to think over. So much had happened since she'd been here as a little girl. Confession. Communion. Her father's funeral. The catechism. Confirmation. And now she was here as an adult in the church. What had it all meant?

It meant everything, she decided.

So she would always be active in the Church. But what kind of adult should she be? It was time to decide. She thought about Papa, bold and active in the world. Mama was stronger than anyone had guessed. She pictured the Sacred Heart teachers and the spinning globe. Missionaries writing from Africa. All the Muslim and Eastern Orthodox students. *All children of God*. Father Zadrima. He had shown her that she could teach.

Gonxha knelt in silence, waiting. There was a pattern. God knew it, and He knew what she should do now that she had grown up. She only needed to be told.

Gonxha yearned for an answer. *Teach*. The thought floated into her mind. That was what she should do. The more she remembered the joy of a classroom, the more sure she was. Where else had she felt that joy? When she pictured herself in Africa. The scenes had come in happy dreams and daytime fantasies. *Dear Lord*, she prayed, *this* is what You wish?

She felt the kneeler shift again as Mama got up. *How can I leave Mama alone?* she asked God. Agatha was going away to school. Lazar was talking about applying to the army. Mama would be alone.

No, she would not. The answer came immediately: Mama would always have the church. Jesus and Mary would be with her. There would always be poor in the neighborhood who needed her help. And Mama's business had grown big and secure.

Gonxha felt light-headed with joy. A missionary teacher! *Thank you, God*, she prayed. He had chosen her path—and He had let her see.

Gonxha found her mother outdoors, wandering in the wildflowers. The shadows were long now. Sunset was only a few moments away. "My little flower bud," Mama said. "Are you rested enough to take the long walk back?"

"Mama," Gonxha began. Her voice sounded solemn, adult. "I am going to be a missionary."

"Is that so?" Mama said, not hearing the seriousness of her daughter's words. She stopped and turned to see if Gonxha was following.

"Mama," Gonxha repeated. "I *am* going to be a missionary. A teacher. In Africa."

"It is going to get dark. We have to move on," Mama scolded. When Gonxha was walking beside her, she leaned over. "You have all the time in the world before you need to make that decision, you know."

Gonxha thought about telling her mother that God had already decided. Instead, she followed Mama silently down the hill toward home.

CHAPTER FOUR

THE CALLING

"Pope Pius XI will canonize a new saint this spring, on May 17, 1925." Gonxha leaned forward in her pew as the priest read an official letter.

A new saint? This year? Who? Fifteen-year-old Gonxha squirmed with excitement. It had been five years since Saint Joan of Arc was canonized along with Saint Gabriel. Now Gonxha was actually going to be a full member of the Church when a new saint was added to the list! The new priest, Father Jambrekovich, let the suspense build in the church.

"Who will be elevated to the list of God's favorites?" he teased. "It is one who was young and fair, simple and honest. One who lost a parent early in life and suffered, then died from weak lungs." Gonxha almost groaned aloud. Who *was* it? Father Zadrima would never have left everyone guessing like this!

"And the answer is . . ." Laughter erupted as people realized what the new priest was doing. Gonxha looked around the church. Everyone was smiling. She decided she really liked Father Jambrekovich. "Therese of Lisieux, the 'Little Flower of Jesus,'" the new priest said, "will become Saint Therese." Many in the congregation murmured their approval. The young French nun had only been dead for twenty-five years or so. Already there were many reports of healings and miracles. "Saint Therese's day will be October first," the priest went on. "We will celebrate her canonization here in May with a great feast."

"And in other news, I would like to invite all Catholic teenagers to join a club I am starting. Are you interested in parties? Outings? Nature walks? We will meet after the service in my office."

Gonxha looked at her mother for permission.

Mama smiled and nodded, then picked up her missal book to read along with the church service. Gonxha opened her own missal and flipped to a section marked with a colored ribbon. It was hard to concentrate through the Mass. A new saint! A new priest who made people laugh in church. And a new club, too?

She joined an eager group of teenagers gathered around Father Jambrekovich. "This club is yours," the priest said. "You can decide how it will be run and what activities you want. . . ." He paused while a few boys chuckled, then added, "Church-approved activities."

Gonxha threw herself into this new club. She helped to run it and offered many ideas for active service. Feeding the poor, raking old people's yards, babysitting during church hours—there were so many things a teenager could do! Other teens suggested parties and trips to Black Mountain, a picnic when it got warmer, and even a trip to watch a new form of entertainment—a moving picture show at the theater.

It was hard to find time for everything. Mama insisted that Gonxha's schoolwork come first. Lazar was away studying on an army scholarship, and Agatha was away at school, too, so Gonxha did all of their household chores as well as her own. There were often extra mouths to feed at the table. "Come to supper," Mama or Gonxha would say to hungry or lonely people they met during the day. "It is no problem for us." This service brought joy to the Bojaxhiu women, but it meant extra cooking and cleanup work later.

The pace didn't bother Gonxha. She kept her life tidy and organized, learning from her mother. Mama decided what was important— the Church, service to others, providing for her family, and prayer—and she did those things well. Nothing else mattered. Gonxha balanced many important things in her life now, but she knew it would only be for a few more years. Then she, too, would go away. Once she had a teaching certificate, she would go to Africa to teach and spread the word of the Church. "Did you know you have a future missionary in your club, Father?" one of the teenagers asked Father Jambrekovich. "That's what Gonxha wants to do."

"No," the priest said. He looked at Gonxha. "You will be a very good ambassador for our faith." The unexpected praise felt like warm sunshine to Gonxha. "I have some magazine articles about missionaries in India. Would you like to read them?"

Gonxha agreed. Learning about workers in other countries might give her tips about her mission in Africa. It did, but not the way Gonxha expected. The women teaching in India were nuns. They had given up everything for Christ. Their lives spent in total service. Gonxha could not read fast enough. These women knew what mattered. How did they do it?

There were no nuns in Skopje. With only one small Catholic church, there was not enough income to support a convent where nuns could live away from other people. Gonxha had never even met a nun. She studied the pictures from India. Some of the nuns wore billowing black and white dresses with stiff hoods and veils. Gonxha had seen many different habits like these in pictures of religious women. Other nuns in India wore *saris*—they wound and draped a long strip of fabric gracefully around their bodies the way Indian women did. *Sari*. Gonxha read the name of this strange garment aloud. She read on.

The conditions in India were as bad as anywhere in Africa. Poverty. Disease. Homelessness. Hunger. And missionaries were there, helping. Gonxha looked up more about India. The country was ruled by the English, and had been for 125 years. The Indians were tired of it. One large religious group, the Hindus, organized to fight for Indian independence. The English helped Indian Muslims form a political party, too. So long as the Muslims and Hindus fought each other, the English thought they could still stay in charge. One man named Gandhi seemed to be the peacemaker the Indians needed. They could win their independence if they all fought together. But the English kept Gandhi in jail—where he couldn't unite the country.

Gonxha checked out books about India from the Skopje library. There were monsoons in the south there, ferocious rainstorms that lasted weeks. When it wasn't raining, the heat was almost unbearable. There were man-eating tigers and deadly cobras. In the north, the vast Himalayan mountains were snow covered year-round.

Leprosy. Tuberculosis. Malaria. Cholera. The list of diseases among the poor went on and on. There was so much sorrow there! Gonxha ached to help somehow. For the first time, she felt her size. Gonxha stood under five feet tall, shorter than most sixth graders. She weighed less than a hundred pounds. What could one tiny woman do in the face of all the needs of the world? India and Indian nuns began to haunt her dreams alongside of Africa.

And another nun was in the news. Sister Therese of Lisieux was about to become a saint. The pope had already made Therese the patroness of missionaries. She had entered the Carmelite Order when she was only fifteen. Gonxha could not get that out of her mind. *She* was fifteen. "Gonxha" meant "little flower," and Therese was known as "the Little Flower" for both her size and her teachings. There were so many connections!

It did not bother Therese that she was small and weak. In her book *The Little Way*, she wrote, "Our Lord does not look so much at the greatness of our actions, nor even at their difficulty, but at the love with which we do them." Gonxha read that book over and over, and another by Therese called *Story of a Soul*.

That book said, "Jesus set the book of nature before me, and I saw that all the flowers he has created are lovely." Gonxha thought of how close she felt to God among the wildflowers of Black Mountain. She read on: "The splendor of the rose and the whiteness of the lily do not rob the little violet of its scent nor the daisy of its simple charm." Gonxha nodded then and almost laughed aloud at Therese's next line: "If every tiny flower wanted to be a rose, spring would lose its loveliness and there would be no wildflowers to make the meadows gay."

Gonxha thought she could bloom very well as a tiny flower somewhere. Perhaps in the fields of India? Father Jambrekovich handed her many more magazines about the missions in India. She spent almost as much time reading for church as she did for schoolwork now.

One day, he said, "Gonxha, I think you and a few other girls would enjoy a sodality." He laughed at her puzzled look and explained, "A sodality is a club for young women who are serious about their faith.

"Gonxha became a leader, as she did in every group she joined. Father brought quotes to the sodality girls to discuss. "'What *have* I done for Christ? What *am* I doing for Christ?

What *will* I do for Christ?'" became one of Gonxha's favorites. "Saint Ignatius Loyola said that," Father Jambrekovich told them. "He helped to found the Jesuit Order of priests."

Loyola was important, Gonxha thought. He began and then ran a whole order of priests. Nuns, monks, and priests led lives within religious communities, but they could be leaders, too. They could run convents or monasteries full of other religious people. They could be teachers and principals in Catholic schools. They could run charities and hospitals. That way, they could do something for the Church *and* the whole world.

But they had to give up so much! Gonxha sighed when she thought about that. Nuns, monks, and priests gave up everything they owned. They could never date or marry. They could not have children. The religious even gave up their independence. They had to agree to let somebody else make all their decisions for them. Poverty. Chastity. Obedience. Those were the three vows every religious person took to serve God. "Could you ever do that?" one of the sodality girls asked Gonxha.

"In a way, it sounds good," Gonxha said slowly. "Giving up everything for Jesus."

It did not sound good to Mama. "Why would you even think about such a thing?" Mama asked. "You are too lively to be a nun," she said. Or, "You aren't healthy enough to live that hard sort of life." And, "Nuns do not get vacations, Little Flower. You could never come home to visit me."

Agatha argued too. "You could be a writer, Gonxha. Look at the articles you have written for the local newspaper! They were about missions in India, and they were good, really good!"

Lazar was no help. "Your life would be wasted in a convent," he wrote. "You should be a political leader like Papa!"

That made Gonxha think about Papa. Politics had killed him. Then she thought about Mama. When Papa was around, Mama's energies went to cooking and cleaning and entertaining his friends. She had spent some time in church activities, of course. But once Papa died, Mama could really devote herself to the church. And to earning money. What if she didn't have to support three children? She could have given all her energies to Jesus.

Suddenly the rule that nuns could not marry made sense. But did Gonxha want that life?

Whenever the church teen group went up to the Letnice chapel, Gonxha prayed about the decision to become a nun. There, in the clear air, it felt right. She talked for hours with Father Jambrekovich about the possibility. He seemed to think becoming a missionary nun was a good idea for her. Gonxha began to research what kinds of nuns were working in India.

The nuns she had read about in the magazines were from the Sisters of Loreto. Their home convent was in Ireland, but they worked in Kolkata, India. The Sisters of Loreto was a teaching order. With them, Gonxha could use her gift as a teacher in a land that called to her. Gonxha looked at a map. Kolkata was huge. It sat right on the Ganges River, where the heat, the monsoon rains, and the poverty were at their worst.

The more she read, the better it sounded. Gonxha knew she could make a difference in the lives of the poor there. She spent hours praying for guidance. She pictured herself wearing the black and white habit. She imagined feeding hungry little Indian children, teaching them to read, and showing them the catechism. She could see their thankful eyes. Joy flooded Gonxha's body. This was what she was made for.

"Mama, I am eighteen now. I have made my decision. I am going to be a nun," she announced in 1928.

Mama sputtered, then put her hand over her mouth. She turned and fled into her bedroom. Then she slammed the door.

Suddenly it was very still in the Bojaxhiu house. "Mama?" Gonxha called softly. No answer.

"Mama, come out. Please?"

Still no answer.

Gonxha put on her coat and wandered down to the church. "Give her time," Father Jambrekovich said. "She needs to pray—and to cry. She is losing a daughter, you know."

"What should I do?" Gonxha asked.

"I will help you apply to the Sisters of Loreto, Gonxha. Then you must wait too. It will be weeks before they decide if they will accept you."

Gonxha mailed the application that afternoon. Father Jambrekovich wrote letters telling the sisters what a leader Gonxha was in the church. He described her deep faith and high energy. He told them she was a top student, a gifted teacher, a real leader, and a thoughtful friend. "Go home and write your news to Lazar and Agatha," the priest told Gonxha. "And keep a hot cup of tea ready for your mama. She will come out of her room— and I think she will be smiling."

It took twenty-four hours, but Mama

opened her door. Her eyes were reddened from crying. She hadn't changed her clothes. She was smiling. Before she said anything at all, Mama hugged Gonxha tightly.

Lazar and Agatha argued through letters. Gonxha's friends began to act differently around her.

"You're going into a *convent*?" one boy said.

"Wonderful!" her sodality girlfriends cheered.

Other people seemed to feel awkward about her calling. Some didn't talk to her. Some spoke carefully around her, apologizing for any curse words that slipped out. It almost felt as if she were already wearing a nun's habit.

At long last, the letter came. She was accepted. After the years of indecision and the weeks of waiting, things began to happen fast. Doctor visits. New underwear. A farewell party. And then suddenly Gonxha was at the train station. She stared at her ticket. September 25, 1928. Skopje to Paris. This was really happening!

All of her relatives crowded around her on the platform. Beyond them it seemed a hundred people had gathered to see her off. The whole church was there. Every sodality member came, and most were wiping their eyes. Father Jambrekovich stood to the side, smiling. The choir sang. Papa's friends came, too, and Mama's good customers—even the Muslims and Orthodox. Gonxha blinked back tears. This was the last time she'd see any of them!

The train whistle blew. Gonxha got onboard with Mama and Agatha. They would travel with her only to a nearby town, Zagreb. Then there would be more good-byes. Gonxha sat by the closest window, trying to see everyone, trying to memorize their faces. As the train pulled away, she rose in her seat and pressed her face to the glass. Gonxha watched Skopje vanish in the distance.

She slid her hand into her pocket and started to pray her Rosary.

CHAPTER FIVE

IRISH NUN

Gonxha rocked with the moving of the train. She stared out the window at passing fields and mountains. For almost four hundred miles she tried to explain herself to her mother. She tried to reassure her sister that she would be fine. And she pretended to sleep so she would not have to answer any more questions. At last the conductor shouted, "Zagreb!" The train pulled into another station. The brakes shrieked, and a puff of steam shot from underneath the car.

A pale young woman stepped onto the train carrying only a small suitcase. She wore the same kind of simple black dress that Gonxha had been told to wear. Her black, soft-soled shoes matched Gonxha's too. "That must be the other one," Mama said. "Your companion on this adventure." Mama and Agatha stood and hugged Gonxha so tightly, she felt her back creak. They stared at one another silently. Everything had been said in the hours on the train. "God bless you," Mama finally said, then her voice began to shake. "I am so proud. . . ."

"There would be no shame if you came home," Agatha said.

Then the Bojaxhius kissed and hugged and wept until the conductor called, "All aboard!" Mama and Agatha hurried off the train as its whistle blew.

"Beitke?" Gonxha called. The girl smiled and strode back to sit beside Gonxha. "I'm glad someone else is going to Loreto," she said.

Beitke's eyes filled with tears. Watching her, Gonxha could feel her eyes watering too. She quickly clasped Beitke's hand and began to chatter. "I can't wait to see the Loreto House in Paris. Our priest said the Mother Superior there will interview us." Beitke didn't answer, so Gonxha tried again. "Do you speak French?"

Beitke shook her head no.

"Oh," Gonxha said. No wonder the girl was so frightened, she thought.

The girls talked little as the train sped through Austria, Germany, and finally into France. A priest met them at the station and drove them to the Loreto House in a new automobile. Gonxha chatted with him a bit, trying out her French. Beitke shrank back on her seat. She seemed about to cry.

The girls stared at a familiar flag when the car stopped by a huge old stone house. Gonxha held her breath as an older man sat down in the front seat.

"Good day, girls. I am from the Yugoslavian embassy," the older man said, straightening his gold braid-edged jacket. He turned to face them. "Mother Superior asked me to translate into Albanian and Serbo-Croat for you this afternoon. I have brought books to help you learn English." He handed each of them a pile of books across the seat back.

"English?" Gonxha stared at him. "I don't know English."

"At missions around the world, girls, the Sisters of the Blessed Virgin Mary speak English," he explained in Albanian. "*When* they speak, that is." He looked at Gonxha. "You do know that your name translated to English is Agnes, don't you?"

"It is?" Gonxha said. "Ag-niss." She tried out the sound of it. "Agnes. I am Agnes. Hello, my name is Agnes."

Beside her on the car seat, Beitke giggled. The girls watched crowded Paris streets pass by until the car pulled up by a fancy doorway. "This is the Loreto center in Paris. Leave your suitcases here," the French priest said from behind the driver's wheel. Gonxha translated for Bienke.

The old embassy staffer knocked softly at the door and whispered with the graceful nun who answered. He turned to the girls and said in Albanian, "Mother Superior Eugene MacAvin is ready for you." As they entered, Gonxha's breath stopped. What if she said something wrong now? Would they send her home? Then she remembered. God had called her. She had nothing to worry about.

"Good day, Agnes," the mother superior said in English. They all stepped into a wood-paneled office. "Good day, Beitke."

Gonxha tried not to stare at the woman while the translator explained what she had said. The nun's kind face was framed in snowy white fabric. A huge white bib covered her chest. It matched white cuffs extending from under a sea of black. Her voice was calm, quiet, controlled. *I will look like that*, Gonxha thought. *I will sound like that*. She shivered with excitement.

"You will go now to Ireland," the mother superior said through the translator. "Other new girls spend their first months as a postulant nun at the Loreto Abby there. They spend a year exploring the history and customs of our order. Your chore will be much simpler. You two will learn English—and quickly. Can you do that?"

As soon as she had heard the old man's

translation, Gonxha knew how to answer. "I already speak four languages, Mother Superior," she said in French. "Latin, Albanian, Serbo-Croat, and, as you can see, French. I enjoy the study."

"That is a good thing, Agnes," the mother superior responded in French. "But do not let yourself be overproud. From this moment on, you will speak nothing but English. Until, that is, you are in India. Then you must master Bengali and one other local language as well."

Gonxha swallowed. "I can do that."

Beside her, Beitke stayed silent.

"Good. The car is waiting to take you to the train. The train will take you to the boat. It is a short sail and another train ride to the Loreto mother house in Ireland." The mother superior stood up. Gonxha's eye caught the enormous crucifix tucked under the nun's belt. A huge Rosary dangled below it.

How beautiful! Gonxha thought. A nun's faith did not have to be hidden away in her pocket.

"Go with God," the mother superior said, and raised her hand to bless the new postulants. The embassy official whisked them away. They were on the train again before Gonxha realized it: She had passed the interview!

Gonxha practiced saying Agnes on the overnight trip. She practiced thinking of herself as Agnes. She practiced *being* Agnes as she studied the English books.

The new Agnes and Beitke tried to learn as many English words as they could the next day. Shadows were falling over the tall, brick front of Loreto Abbey in Rathfarnsham, Ireland, as they arrived. The sunset glinted off four stories' worth of windows, but there seemed to be no life inside. Beitke and Agnes climbed out of the car stiffly. The heavy wooden convent door swung open as they approached.

"I am Mother Mary Borgia Irwin," a nun introduced herself quietly in English. "You are?"

Even though Agnes could not speak

English, she could tell the woman had asked a question. She guessed at the answer. "Agnes Bojaxhiu," she said politely.

The nun smiled and turned to Beitke. Agnes ached to help her new friend. But helping her would mean saying a few words in Albanian. She was not supposed to do that here. Finally Beitke said her own name. "Come," the nun said, just above a whisper. She led them off toward a huge set of stairs. Agnes stared at her movement. Mother Mary Borgia Irwin did not bob as she walked. She did not sway or twist, dip or rock. Instead, she seemed to float silently across the floor. She floated up the stairs, too, holding the hem of her black habit so it just missed each step.

I will walk like that, Agnes thought. Questions threatened to bubble out of her. *Where is everyone? Where will I sleep? Is there a supper for me? Where is a bathroom?*

As if she had heard, Mother Mary Borgia Irwin waved a hand toward an open door. "Bathroom," she said distinctly. Behind the door stood a toilet and a little sink. Agnes gasped with relief, but looked at Beitke for permission before she ducked inside.

Bathroom, she said the English word to herself. *Bathroom*. Agnes washed her hands and lifted her head to glance into the mirror. But there was no mirror over the sink. She looked around the little room. No rug, no window, no color, no flowers, and *no* mirror.

She sighed and let Beitke use the bathroom. In the hall, Agnes asked about food by raising her hand to her mouth. Mother Mary Borgia Irwin nodded and said clearly, "You will eat." Her eyes flicked toward the bathroom door. "Wait." As soon as Beitke came out, Mother Irwin said, "Bedroom," and led them to a little room with two beds. There was an identical table by each, where large squares of black cloth lay folded neatly. Last, a pull curtain hung between the beds.

"Bedroom," Agnes repeated the new English word. As she put her suitcase on one bed, Mother Irwin unfolded the smooth black cloth.

"Your veil," she said. "The other girls got theirs last week." As Agnes stood quietly listening to the strange language, the nun draped the veil over her head. Its front edge lay just along Agnes's hairline. Next, Mother Irwin smoothed the edges down over Agnes's ears and crossed them at the back of her neck. It took a single straight pin to hold the veil together. "There," she said. "Do not shake your head." She showed what she meant and moved on to Beitke's veil. The girls looked at each other and grinned. Mother Irwin made a quiet *tch* sound to end their silliness and hurried them to the chapel.

The pews were filled with row after row of nuns. Each sat upright, head bowed, eyes down, hands hidden. It was perfect, Agnes thought. Perfect for Jesus. Every one of those women lived just for Him.

"Amen," a woman's voice came from the side. The silence was broken by the whispers of moving cloth and a tiny, stifled sneeze. Mother Irwin slid into the back pew, and the girls followed. Chains clinked, and suddenly the entire room began saying the Rosary in unison. Agnes pulled hers out and fingered the crucifix. The nuns were saying their Rosaries in English, so she could not join in—at least not yet. The beads were the same, though, as well as the mysteries. Hail Mary was always repeated ten times in a row. It made those words easy for Agnes to learn. She almost had the Our Father prayer memorized, too, by the time the nuns all said, "Amen."

Silently, they rose, bowed, blessed themselves, and filed out of the chapel. Agnes was filled with their beauty. She felt like she was soaring, until her stomach grumbled. Beitke looked her way and grinned, but no other nun seemed to notice.

In the dining room, silent nuns sat at long tables. Agnes sat down quietly in the first open seat. The nun beside her passed a large bowl. There were no grape leaves inside. No lamb or cinnamon-and-garlic scent. The bowl held heaping piles of white paste. Agnes put some on her plate just as the others did. The next bowl held large, boiled leaves that smelled sour. Bits of pink meat floated in the greasy water. Agnes took a helping of this, too, since there didn't seem to be anything else but water for dinner.

The white paste tasted almost like mashed chickpeas that someone forgot to season. The leaves were tart and filling. The pink meat added a salty flavor. Agnes just wished she knew what she was eating.

After the meal they went back to the chapel to pray and then up to bed. Agnes put on the simple white nightgown she had been told to bring. She brushed her teeth, knelt to say her prayers, and then lay awake under a thin blanket. Strange-sounding English words and strange-tasting Irish food floated through her mind. A sniffling sound came through the thin curtain from Beitke's side of the room. It made Agnes remember Mama, waving good-bye. She imagined her friends at the railroad station. Stop it, Agnes scolded herself. She practiced saying Hail Marys in English until finally she fell asleep.

Brrrrrring! A loud buzzer startled Agnes awake. She dressed and followed a silent line of nuns to chapel, then listened through a sweet chant. Then she went to Mass and to breakfast. Afterward came chapel again, then English lessons, then more chapel, then lunch. In the afternoon there were English lessons before prayer and the Rosary in the chapel. Supper came next, then chapel, then bed. Except for Mother Irwin, no nun spoke to her. No one smiled. No one even met her eyes.

Agnes spent the day walking silently from one place to another with Mother Irwin and Beitke. If there were other postulants at Loreto Abby, she never met them. Her only chores seemed to be worshipping God—and learning English.

After a few days, the schedule began to make sense. So did the prayers and practice conversations with Mother in the classroom, where they could speak aloud. Agnes began to recognize different nuns, too. She longed to sing with their choir. Such voices! A month went by before she felt strong enough in her English to ask about the choir.

"No," Mother Irwin said. "There is no time. Tomorrow you leave for India."

"Tomorrow?" Agnes's voice sounded very loud to her. "India?!" Now it rose to a squeak.

Mother gave her a quick frown. "Yes. You and Beitke will go with three other sisters. They are from the Franciscan Order. There is no priest on the ship."

Agnes's breath caught. *The ship? This is really happening.* It would take two months to get to India. On a *ship*. The voice within her mind rose to a squeak too.

"No priest," Mother reminded them, "means there will be no confession and no Mass for either of you for months. Treasure your chapel time tomorrow, girls."

Agnes swallowed hard. Since first Communion, she had attended Mass almost every morning. She had confessed to a priest every week. How could this be?

As soon as they boarded the *Marchait*, the Franciscan nuns set up a daily prayer schedule with Agnes and Beitke. Launching in October, the boat carried them the length of the Mediterranean Sea, through the Suez Canal, along the Red Sea, and then across the Indian Ocean. By Christmas, the girls could smell land. "Flowers. Spices and flowers," Agnes said after a deep breath.

"Animals." Beitke wrinkled her nose. "And garbage."

"We will stop at the island of Ceylon," the captain told them. "We need to refuel for the last week's sail to India. You may go ashore, if you like. And we are taking on a special Christmas gift for you."

The girls could not guess what their gift was. Finally, they saw a priest stride up the gangplank from Ceylon. "Mass," breathed Agnes.

"Confession," Beitke said.

"Merry Christmas," the captain said. Then he gave the orders to raise anchor again. "Next stop, Madras, India," he told the nuns. "You all should go ashore there. You will see what you've gotten yourself into."

Once they docked, Agnes froze at the top of the gangplank. She could not make her feet take her into the swirling, stinking mass of people on the dock at Madras. As she stared, bits of the noisy scene made sense. A family of little children slept on the bare, wooden wharf. Crippled beggars raised their hands toward the ship. Some had no fingers. Others had no legs. Garbage lay in piles, and cattle wandered loose in the street. One bull raised his tail and squirted hot, stinking puddles of waste on the road. No one seemed to notice.

And skin! Naked skin showed everywhere. Men walked about bare-chested. Some were bare-legged, as well, dressed only in cloth at the waist. Agnes tried not to look. She had never even seen her own brother's legs. All the skin she saw here gleamed brown or honey-colored, cinnamon or tan in the harsh sunshine. She took a breath. Sweat.

India, she told herself. *This is where God wants me to be.* She made herself walk down the gangplank, but had to jump back. A half-naked man ran past, panting as he pulled a two-wheeled cart. A rich woman sat inside, looking bored.

"That is a rickshaw," the priest said, stopping behind Agnes. "This all takes a while to get used to," he said gently. "But you will come to love it."

Agnes stared at a woman lying on the dirt. She was groaning and calling out. Agnes supposed she was begging for help in her own language. Nobody stopped. Crowds pushed this way and that. Earrings and nose rings glinted above necklaces of bright yellow gold. The fabrics came in brighter colors than even Mama could buy, Agnes thought. Women wore *saris,* just like in the magazine pictures.

"Jesus is here," the priest said. He looked at the sick woman with Agnes. "He is here—and he needs you."

Agnes remembered the Bible verse: "Whatsoever you do for one of the least of these, my brothers, you do for me." She gazed about. "But, Father, there is so much need here!"

"That is why you have come," he said.

Two days later they landed in Calcutta, India's largest city. It was hotter, dirtier, poorer, and more crowded than Madras. This time, Agnes was ready. She knew to look for Jesus' suffering face in these people. How she loved Jesus! That love washed over the whole scene. Calcutta was still dirty. It still stank. But now the city called to her.

A pair of Loreto sisters met them at the dock. "We can only stay at the convent here a week," they told Agnes and Beitke. "Then we will take a train to the convent in Darjeeling. That is the home where you will be trained as sisters of the Blessed Virgin Mary."

"Is Darjeeling like Calcutta?" Agnes asked.

"No, no," they said. "It is smaller and cooler and cleaner. It is hundreds of miles north of here, up near the Himalayan mountains."

After a week surrounded by Loreto sisters who neither smiled nor spoke, the rhythm of the train clacking along tracks felt good to Agnes. She was going to a new home. Rice paddies and water buffalo flashed by the windows. Handsome English mansions rose skyward one moment. The next scene showed mud huts and half-naked laborers. There didn't seem to be any middle class in India between wealth and poverty.

In Darjeeling, a Loreto sister greeted them at the train station. Agnes thought she looked clean and calm and holy. "I expect you could use a bath," the sister said to the girls. "My name is Sister Baptista Murphy. I am in charge of the postulates. That means you." There was a sparkle in this nun's eyes that made Agnes like her immediately.

"There is a rule for every little thing in the convent," Sister Baptista Murphy told the girls.

"Oh, good," Agnes said. The nun waited for

an explanation. "I like to know exactly what I'm supposed to do. Following rules helps me to be good. Now that I am here, I want to be the perfect nun for Jesus."

"We will see," said Sister Murphy. "One of the first rules of our order is to pray always. You can't do that if you are talking to someone besides Jesus. That is why we observe silence."

"What if we see a fire?" Beitke asked.

"For safety or for health, you may speak. You may greet a fellow postulant in passing in the hall. And you may talk together as needed while doing chores. Now, do you want that bath?"

Both girls nodded. Sister Murphy pointed down the hall toward the shower room. "We walk slowly, evenly, and silently," she said. "We don't want to disturb anyone's prayer." Then she showed them how to walk as if they were floating. "Head up, Agnes," the sister cautioned. "Don't swing your shoulders, Beitke. Or your hips. Not even a little."

"Agnes, you are brushing your hands

against your skirts. Hold them still as you walk. Now go back to the bedroom and try it again." She watched closely. "Better. Better. But, Beitke, you are slouching now. Stand straight."

"Agnes, are you part bunny rabbit? Do not bounce with each step. Go back again and set each foot flat against the ground. Take slightly smaller steps. See? Now you are floating."

Agnes slumped in relief. She had done it!

"Stand straight!" Sister Baptista Murphy scolded. "There is another rule." Both girls looked at her. "You must not *do* that, ladies. Do not look at me. Or anyone else. Keep your eyes looking downward focused about four feet in front of you."

They all walked back to the bedroom again and picked up their toothbrushes, deodorant, and soap. "Eyes down, head up, feet flat, shoulders straight," the sister kept up a steady list of reminders on the way to the shower room. "You are behind the other postulants," Sister Baptiste Murphy said. "So I must rush this.

The eyes, girls. Don't look at me. It is called Custody of the Eyes. We don't speak so our minds are always free to pray. We don't look around, either, so we won't be distracted from God."

Beitke sighed.

"No sighs, sniffles, burps, grunts, yawns, or lip-smacking," the sister said. Then she was quiet for a moment. "You have come so far to get here, girls. Forgive me. I should not be rushing you. Not yet. I will have your hoods ready when you have washed."

Agnes and Beitke showered silently, exhausted. They both tried to float back to their bedroom, eyes down. Agnes tripped and Beitke ran into her and they both collapsed in giggles. "Supper will not wait." The girls looked up to see Sister Murphy standing, stern, in the doorway.

"Sorry, Sister," they mumbled as they pulled themselves together.

Both stood straight and silent as Sister removed their veils. She settled black hoods on their heads and tied them with black ribbons at their necks. "These are coifs," she told them. "They keep stray hairs away from your face where they might distract you." Finally she put their veils back on. The girls looked at each other, then quickly dropped their eyes. Agnes felt her face redden. In that quick glimpse, she had seen what she must look like.

Nothing was left of Gonxha Bojaxhiu. In her place floated a postulant of the Sisters of the Blessed Virgin Mary.

CHAPTER SIX
A CALL WITHIN A CALL

Agnes loved all the rules she learned as a postulant. She knew that following them would make her holy. She would be closer to Jesus. Even when the rules seemed to make no sense at all, she obeyed them. Sooner or later she always saw their wisdom. Agnes was shocked when Sister Baptista Murphy said, "Do not have particular friendships."

"Particular?" Agnes wondered at the strange choice of words. Didn't everyone have a best friend? she thought. Agnes felt a special bond with Beitke. They had traveled together. Their beds were side by side. They had learned English together.

To follow this new rule, Agnes stopped sitting with Beitke at every mealtime. She stopped remembering funny things to tell her the next time they washed dishes or peeled potatoes together. She stopped paying so much attention to her friend.

Instead, Agnes tried speaking to every single postulant. Some of them she liked, some she didn't. She sat with anyone, walked next to anyone, and folded laundry with anyone. She didn't get into deep, personal talks, but had a few kind words for every girl. All of the girls tried to follow the same rule.

In a few days Agnes could see the difference. Now there was no popular girl. There were no cliques. There was no one sitting alone at a table, either. Agnes knew a bit about every one of the postulants in her class. And everyone knew a little about her, too. "You are all equal in God's eyes," Sister Baptista Murphy said. "Now you are acting as if you believe it."

It was months before Agnes felt the deeper point of that rule. When she was lonely, she had no best friend to tell. She had no special friend to celebrate with, either. When she was tired or angry, sad or confused, there wasn't anyone who really understood her—except Jesus. Agnes prayed her heart out to God, to Jesus, and to Mary. She found friendship and comfort there too. "Pray constantly," Sister Murphy had told her.

Some of the postulants could not adjust to life as a nun. It was too hard. There were too many rules. They missed their families. They wanted to get married. Those women quietly dropped out of the postulant's class. Nobody spoke of them again.

By the end of Agnes's year as a postulant, the rules had become habits. The schedules made sense. Agnes knew she loved the Loreto Sisters and was ready to take the next step.

After Mass on the morning of May 24, 1929, Agnes and all the postulates that were left filed into a meeting room. One by one, they took off their black veils and coifs. Sister Baptista Murphy cut off the long, beautiful hair they'd kept hidden. Locks of red and yellow, brown and black fell to the floor. Straight, curly, thick, or fine, it all was gone. Nothing was left but a raggedy fringe.

Sister Baptista showed them how to put on the huge white collar that covered their shoulders and dipped almost to their waist in front. Now a belt held their habits tight at the waist. In place of the hoodlike coif, each girl got a stiff wimple. This large, white head covering went from the forehead, down the cheeks, to fasten under the chin. Last, Sister Baptista Murphy brought out veils of sparkling white.

"By what name will you be known?" an Archbishop asked the new, snow white novices as they stood in the chapel. Agnes was ready with her answer. She would take the name of the saint who meant the most to her, the "Little Flower," Therese of Lisieux, France. But Agnes chose to use the English spelling.

"Sister Mary Teresa of the Child Jesus," the archbishop repeated the name Agnes had chosen. Her heart nearly burst with joy. If she had stayed in Yugoslavia, Mama, Lazar, and Agatha would have been there to celebrate. Members of her old sodality might have come, and Father Jambrekovich, too. They would have brought gifts and shared a feast. Instead, the newly named Sister Teresa shared her joy with her sisters and with Jesus.

She still had two years as a novice before she took her vows. The first year, she studied the Bible. She learned the constitution of her order and its rule books. Sister Teresa also took a closer look at the vows she would be asked to take.

Poverty had many meanings. As a nun, Sister Teresa would own nothing. Her clothing, her toothbrush, even her underwear belonged to the order. Any money she earned or received had to be passed right back to the convent. All of her time belonged to the order, too. Her accomplishments were not her own either. They were all due to the love of God.

Sister Teresa knew why nuns could not marry. That would split their time and energy away from the Church. "Think of taking your vows as actually marrying Jesus," Sister

Baptista reminded the class. That made sense to Sister Teresa. Jesus was her best friend. In prayer and in service, he brought her the greatest joy. He protected and comforted her. And Agnes loved him with all her heart.

Chastity meant more than not getting married. It meant that Sister Teresa had to keep her body healthy as well as pure. There was no silk underwear to feel good on her skin. Her showers were short and often cold. Nuns did not hug each other in celebration or wipe away each other's tears. "If you ever brush against another sister in passing," Sister Murphy told the novices, "ask her forgiveness immediately."

"Now we will speak of obedience," Sister Murphy began one lecture. Sister Teresa sat tall and straight in her seat, listening closely. Sister Murphy was an excellent teacher. Sister Teresa needed to know about obedience, of course. She also needed to learn about teaching. Sister Baptista always broke complicated things down until everyone could understand them. She was patient. She was very firm. She showed Christian love for her students without touching, praising too much, or going easy on anyone.

Sister Teresa sometimes imagined herself teaching in the slums of Calcutta. Dozens of half-naked children circled her. They listened to every word she said. They learned to read. They learned to write. And they learned their catechism perfectly because Sister Teresa was firm and loving, like Sister Murphy.

Now that she was a novice, Sister Teresa spent more time with the older nuns. She listened as they spoke of their mother superior, the nun in charge of the convent. She managed a budget, a huge kitchen, the gardens, a school, an infirmary, and more. Each department in the convent had a nun in charge. They all reported to the mother superior. A different mother superior ran each convent of the Sisters of the Blessed Virgin Mary. There were dozens of convents. Finally, there was a single nun, the superior general, in charge of the order, worldwide.

Sister Teresa remembered the joy of leading

church clubs in high school. She thought about her own papa. He was a leader among revolutionaries. Mama led a small business all by herself. But these nuns? They led whole cities of women in the service of God!

What would I have become, Sister Teresa wondered sometimes, *if I had stayed in little Skopje?* Women were not allowed to run for political office there. They could not be police-women, lawyers, builders, or plumbers. Women were never painters or scientists. *I could have been a teacher*, she thought. *I could have been a nurse. I could have been a secretary like Agatha. I could have gotten married.*

"Thank you, Jesus," she prayed silently as she scrubbed carrots or ironed habits or swept bathrooms. "I thank you for the chance to use all my talents."

Sister Teresa was singing in the choir again. She was at the top of her classes, though no one ever mentioned it. She was surrounded by role models in leadership and holiness. And she knew just where she was headed.

But she needed to learn obedience. "You must be obedient in all things," Sister Murphy told the novices. "The rules must be followed. You must eat when and what you are told to and not one bit more. You must wear what we tell you to, act by the rules, and obey every order without pause. There will be no argument."

There was none. Sister Teresa longed to be a perfect nun. She jumped to help in the convent's hospital when she was told to. She met Indians there, sick and needy. "What a state they are in!" she wrote for the *Catholic Missions* magazine. "On their backs are lumps and lesions, among the numerous ulcers. . . . Later, a woman with a broken arm . . . then comes a boy who has been stabbed in the back. . . . Finally a man arrives with a bundle from which two dry twigs protrude. They are the legs of a child." Sister Teresa learned how to help them in the hospital. First she smiled to show them her love.

A few more of the novices went home. Not Sister Teresa.

"Sister, will you step in to teach a class?" When asked, Sister Teresa said yes, obediently, though she wasn't speaking Bengali very well yet. She was learning the Hindi language, too, as she had been told. Sister Teresa knew she would need to speak both languages on the streets of Calcutta. In the classroom, she learned to look at the students. Keeping her gaze downward worked fine in the convent. It would help her stay focused in the city. But children needed to know she was watching everything they did. And they needed to see her smile.

On May 24, 1931, Sister Mary Teresa of the Child Jesus took her first vows of poverty, chastity, and obedience. She could renew these vows yearly until she was ready to take the Final Vows that would last until she died. The archbishop slid a simple ring onto her right hand to remind her and everyone else that she was promised only to Jesus. She changed her white veil for a black one and awaited her orders.

"You will go to Calcutta," the mother superior said.

With a last look at the Himalayan mountains, Sister Teresa boarded a train to the hot, crowded, poor city of her dreams. When she got to Entally, a neighborhood in Calcutta, a local priest welcomed her at the station. "You will teach at Loreto Entally," he said, driving her to the convent.

Inside, the local mother superior welcomed her again and said, "This is Mother Cenacle. She is the principal of both of our high schools here. One school is for English girls. The other is for Bengali girls."

Sister Teresa walked behind Mother Cenacle to see where she would be working. The first school was bright and clean. The students were all the children of rich English families. They looked healthy and well dressed. They spoke English.

An identical Bengali school stood across a broad green lawn. Rich Indian children studied in light, airy classrooms. Palm trees and flowering bushes made the twin schools seem like a garden. A high wall, painted a pretty light blue, surrounded the Loreto schools and the convent where the nuns lived. It kept the smell and poverty and danger of Calcutta out.

"You will teach geography in the English school," the Mother Superior said. "Later we will add history."

This was not what Sister Teresa had expected. She wanted the adventure of the streets. She longed for the thrill of success against high odds. But God and the school principal had other ideas.

"Yes, Mother," Sister Teresa said obediently.

That morning, she moved into the school. The prayer schedule was the same there. The rules of behavior were too. But the sisters were not cloistered away, locked inside a quiet convent. This was a boarding school. Sister Teresa was used to seeing only other nuns and one priest every morning to say Mass. Now there were teenage girls around, night and day.

The energy that Sister Teresa's students brought her seemed to be a gift from God. They questioned and teased and laughed aloud. They learned, but they challenged. When they came to class, they brought jokes and news with them.

In 1927, the news was bad. In Germany, a new leader was taking power. Adolf Hitler threatened everyone who was not like him. That meant the Roman Catholics in the country were in danger. The new Nazi party seemed to hate Jews and Gypsies, too, dark-skinned people, the elderly, the sick, and the simple-minded. Sister Teresa prayed for all those people.

There were also problems in India. Tempers had reached a boiling point. Hindus and Muslims were tired of being ruled by the British Empire. Riots had broken out. Gandhi was still in jail, along with thirty-five thousand of his followers. Still, his influence spread across the land. "Fight," he told his followers, "but not with violence. Fight with the force of truth!"

There was no fighting inside the peaceful

blue walls. Sister Teresa loved teaching, and the students loved her, too. The other teachers came to respect the tiny nun's skill and knowledge. Soon she was asked to help in other areas of the school. She planned student events and helped younger teachers. Some of her students started coming to her for personal advice.

Sister Teresa could have forgotten the poverty and need outside the wall, except for one thing. She could look down into the street from her bedroom window. Every night after she said her prayers, she watched beggars crawl by. She saw rats stealing food from children. She heard sobbing.

By 1935, Sister Teresa was twenty-five and doing far more than just teaching at Loreto Entally. She nursed the sick at the infirmary. She helped other nuns with their studies. She wrote magazine articles for international Church magazines. She often wrote about the poor. Year after year she renewed her vows, though some of the other novices dropped out. Every year Sister Teresa was allowed a week away to retreat in prayer. She always spent her week in the slums of Calcutta.

One day, Mother Cenacle asked, "Would you like to spend your Sunday afternoons teaching a free day school here in the convent? We have an old chapel that is just being used for storage. . . ." The mother superior explained her plans. Rich parents paid for the boarding school students to go to Loreto Entally. At this new day school, poor children would be welcome for free.

"I will do it," Sister Teresa said, breathing a prayer of thanks to Jesus.

The first Sunday, fifty little children came to the day school out of curiosity. They stayed, staring at the tiny nun who brought a bucket and a broom and swabbed the floors clean. They began to help, moving desks and chairs. Some washed windows. Sister Teresa could not hope to learn all of their names at once. Instead, she made a point to smile at each one and touch them. "They began to leap and sing only when I put my hand on each dirty little head," she wrote for *Catholic Missions* magazine. The children called her Ma, a Bengali word that meant "Mama."

More children came the next week. Still more flooded the little day school after that. Soon there were hundreds of children calling her Ma. When other nuns began helping at the day school, Sister Teresa asked Mother Cenacle, "May I go outside for a few hours? I want to see the children's homes. I want to meet their parents."

Usually, the nuns were not allowed to leave the Loreto enclosure unless on retreat or official business. Mother Cenacle checked with the priests and her own superior. It took weeks, but finally Sister Teresa had permission to go beyond the clean blue wall to see where her poor students lived.

It was worse than she'd thought. She found whole families living in single rooms. The ceilings were so low that even Sister Teresa could not stand upright. They slept on the floor. When their begging went well, they could afford to eat rice. When people gave them nothing, their landlords threw them out. But each family welcomed Sister Teresa with her big, kind smile.

On May 24, 1937, Sister Teresa boarded the train to Darjeeling again. This time she made her Final Vows. Before the bishop she promised poverty, chastity, and obedience to the Order of the Blessed Virgin Mary for the rest of her life. There was no backing out now. The rules said she was a Loreto nun forever, only now she was called Mother Teresa instead of "Sister."

When she got home to Entally, Mother Cenacle had surprising news. "I have been assigned to another job," Mother Cenacle told her.

"We will miss you," Sister Teresa told her. She knew Mother would leave the school she loved without a complaint. Like Mother Teresa, she was a professed nun and had promised to instantly obey any order she was given.

"You, my little flower," Mother Cenacle said, "you will be mother superior over the school in my place."

"Yes, Mother," Mother Teresa said, though her head was spinning. Could she do this huge job? Be a principal over the teachers and students of two girls' boarding schools and the day school, too? She had only been with the Loreto sisters for seven years. Mother Teresa glanced down at her ring. *Jesus will help me*, she thought, and calm flooded through her.

Now she organized other nuns to do the work instead of doing it all herself. Her own mama had taught her to handle many tasks. She had also learned from the nuns in Darjeeling and by watching Mother Cenacle. Though she was only twenty-six, she was ready for leadership.

Being a mother superior meant that she worked more closely with the priests. Through the years there had always been priests to whom she confessed. Some had given her good advice. Others had helped her with problems in faith. Now Father Henry helped her with a sodality at Loretto Entally for the girls in grades six and up. "Instead of just meeting at the school," he suggested, "couldn't your girls volunteer out beyond the walls?"

There was a problem with this. Because of her vows, Mother Teresa could not leave the school grounds. "It would be so good for these rich English girls to see how most Indians live," she said. "Can they go alone?" She talked it over with Father Henry. In the end, they let small groups of girls go out together. Sometimes the sodality girls visited neighborhoods on the Hindu side of the school. Other times they went out into the Muslim area on the other side. Each time, Mother Teresa worried. She also wished she could join them.

A letter arrived from her mama that summer. It had been eleven years since they had hugged good-bye on the train. Mother Teresa expected congratulations for her job promotion. Instead, Mama Bojaxhiu wrote, "Dear child, do not forget that you went out to India for the sake of the poor." It made Mother Teresa think. She was moving up the ladder of church positions. That was good for herself and for her order—but it didn't feed the hungry. She was doing wonderful things for her students. But they came from rich English and Indian families. The day school was still helping underprivileged children, but Mother Teresa did not teach there anymore. She was too busy managing the whole community to take time for the poor.

God had called her to India to reach the poor. She was not doing God's will. And she had taken permanent vows to stay with the Sisters of the Blessed Virgin Mary. What could she do?

She couldn't think of an answer. She didn't have to. Suddenly her time was taken up protecting her nuns while war broke out. Hitler's armies began fighting all over Europe. In Italy, the pope wanted peace, but Benito Mussolini won elections in Italy. He joined forces with Hitler to conquer other countries. The Japanese declared war in the Pacific, too. They attacked China. They bombed Hawaii at Pearl Harbor. And on April 6, 1942, the Japanese bombed Madras, India. Then they marched toward Calcutta.

English soldiers took over space at the Loreto Entally. Mother Teresa had to find room for them and for her nuns and the students, too. She had to find food for everyone to eat. It wasn't easy. Hindus and Muslims fought against each other and the English. Blood spattered the streets of Calcutta. Starvation swept India along with the World War. Sickness followed. Overworked Mother Teresa came down with tuberculosis.

On September 10, 1946, Mother Teresa boarded a train to Darjeeling for her yearly retreat. It was a Loreto rule. Nuns needed a break for physical and spiritual health—even in the middle of a war. Mother Teresa was too obedient to argue. She was also exhausted. She had wandered out into the violence alone to find food for her girls. She had held her nuns together as they heard dreadful news about their families back home. Mother Teresa had done the impossible, keeping an island of calm in the middle of the war. But inside, she was far from calm.

She was ill and feverish. "You must rest on this retreat," they had told her. She coughed and pressed a hand to her forehead. *Can you take your own temperature that way?* she wondered. She did not even have the energy to smile. Feeling sick made everything seem hopeless.

On the way to the mountains, the *click-clack* of the train's wheels did not put her to sleep. The endless rice fields outside the windows did not bring her peace. The retreat was not solving her problem. She was *not* following God's will! The roar of the train's engine seemed to grow louder and louder. Mother Teresa's prayers were frantic. *What should I do, Jesus? Tell me what to do!*

Suddenly a calm came over her. A shaft of sunlight made the train compartment glow. Mother Teresa trembled, listening for Jesus' reply. At first there was nothing. Then, clearly, over the engine sounds, He answered:

"Go to the poor."

Mother Teresa closed her eyes, but the strange glow filtered through her eyelids. Incredibly, Jesus' voice went on. He was sitting right beside her! "Leave the convent," he said. "Live with the poorest of the poor." She opened her eyes. There he was, tall and strong.

"How can I?" Mother Teresa's voice trembled.

"You came all the way to India," His voice echoed on in the engine roar. "Are you afraid to go one more step with me?" The train ducked into a tunnel. For a moment, all was dark. Then suddenly the train burst out of the other end of the tunnel. Sunlight filled the car.

There was no one in the seat beside Mother Teresa. She held her breath, listening for His voice. Her body tingled all over. Saints had miracles. The holiest had seen visions. And now Jesus had visited little Gonxha of Skopje. She remembered to breathe. Then she began shuddering.

God had spoken.

She had no choice but to obey.

CHAPTER SEVEN

THE POOREST OF THE POOR

Leave the convent? Live with the poorest of the poor? Mother Teresa had no idea how she could do this. She had vowed to give her life to Jesus—but as a Loreto nun. She had to live in one of their convents. But she had heard Jesus' request just as clearly as if he were riding in the train car with her.

During the retreat, she prayed for guidance. She meditated. She paced and worried and prayed some more. A plan began to form. She could do this, if she had God's help. Her health improved as the medicines worked.

Back home in Calcutta, she told her priest that she had heard from Jesus. She handed him a written report with all the details of the miracle. It included the plan she had made.

"You?" Father Van Exem said. "Alone on the streets of Calcutta? We must pray on this."

She was just as firm when she told Archbishop Ferdinand Périer when he visited the school months later. "You are asking to leave the Order of the Blessed Virgin Mary?" he asked, stunned. "But you still want to be a nun? And wear a *sari*? On the streets alone?" He left, saying he would pray on it.

Mother Teresa knew the problem would probably involve every level of church leadership. It would have to be taken to the pope. He was in charge of all of the Catholic churches on Earth. Under him were cardinals, priests who led several countries each. Archbishops came next. Archbishop Périer was in charge of all of India's Catholic churches. Under him came the bishops, responsible for different sections of the country. The priests were only in charge of one church and the Catholics living around it.

"You must go to a medical center," Father Van Exem said weeks later. "Perhaps you have some sickness that has caused you to change so much." She knew the archbishop must have told him what she had heard and decided. Obediently, she went for testing. The doctors could find nothing wrong with Mother Teresa.

Back at the Entally school, Mother Teresa threw herself into her job as mother superior. She spent more and more time with the sodality girls. Some were from the Bengali building; some were English. They all loved their God— and they loved Mother Teresa. "What have you *done* for Jesus?" she challenged them. "What are you *doing* for Jesus? What *will* you do for Jesus?"

She smiled from the doorway as they went out onto the streets to help the poor. "Tell me everything," she said as they returned with tales of hunger and squalor and disease. They talked about ways to help. Then, the next time the sodality girls left, they took food, and soap, and medicine and Ma's big smile with them.

The archbishop got back to Mother Teresa with a suggestion. "The Daughters of St. Anne are Bengali women who already work in the city. Can you work with them?" Mother Teresa tried, but the Daughters already had their own rules and history. They did not want to change for a foreign nun, even one as holy as Mother Teresa.

"I will write a letter to the pope asking permission for you to start a new order," the archbishop said. "You will have to be patient. You will also have to write asking the superior general of the Loreto Sisters to release you from your vows."

Mother Teresa did as she was told. Another year passed. India split into two free countries; Pakistan for the Muslims, and India for the Hindu. India's beloved wise man, Gandhi, was out of jail now. He went on a hunger strike, vowing not to eat until all violence stopped. No one wanted him to die, so peace came to Calcutta. Then Gandhi was murdered, and the fighting began again.

In August of 1948, the archbishop brought Mother Teresa good news. "You are now a nun without an order," he said. "You have one year to prove your new 'Missionaries of Charity' Order can succeed, or you must return to the Loreto Entally and teach."

Mother Teresa wasted no time. She arranged for extra medical training at the Holy Family Hospital in nearby Patna. The nursing nuns there were thrilled with her new ideas and they helped with whatever they could.

She showed them the *sari* her Sisters of Charity would wear over simple white dresses. "*Saris* will work," the nurses said. "But they will have to be washed every day." Mother Teresa made a plan for that.

"My order will eat nothing but rice and salt, just as the poorest of the poor do," Mother Teresa said. The nurses told her how unhealthy that would be. They explained what a human body must have to stay strong enough to help others.

"And think of the stress of the work you will do!" another nurse said. "Your nuns must go on retreats every year—and they will need a break every week, too." Mother Teresa had not thought of this.

She shared more of her plans. "We will be converting souls to Jesus as we ease their suffering. We can teach the catechism and baptize people into the Church."

"Focus on physical needs first," an experienced nurse said. "You can't do everything." Back and forth the ideas flew while Mother Teresa helped care for victims with smallpox, malaria, and leprosy. She learned to clean bedpans, wash patients, give injections, and soothe fears. Record keeping was important. So was hand washing. By the time Mother Teresa left for Calcutta's slums, she knew what she needed to do. As a going away gift, the nursing nuns gave her a pair of sturdy sandals.

For the next two weeks she stayed with the Little Sisters of the Poor. They ran the St. Joseph's Home for the Aged in Calcutta. She studied how to make very old people comfortable. She learned about their special medical needs. She walked out every day into the city, exploring the neighborhoods.

On December 21, 1948, more than two years after she'd heard Jesus' call, Mother Teresa started her work. She had rented a tiny room for herself to live in and had a few rupees for food. Other than that, she had faith, and love, and a wide, friendly smile.

She decided to start with a school. It wasn't hard to gather five curious little children to an empty lot beside a weedy pond named Moti Jhil. After all, she looked so strange. What was a tiny foreign woman doing wearing a *sari*? She had no stockings on either. And she had sandals on her feet!

Mother Teresa began by scratching Bengali letters into the dirt with a stick. She let the children try, and praised them when their letters were perfect. She taught them a simple song. She clearly loved them. "Come back to Moti Jhil tomorrow," she said.

They did, and they brought their friends. Mother Teresa rinsed the dirt off each child with water from the pond. She taught them the alphabet. She told them to say "please" and "thank you" and to take turns. And she praised every success. These beggar children were used to being kicked and spit at. Mother Teresa smiled at them instead.

A man walking by watched for a moment, then gave her a coin. More coins came in as the day passed. "Can you spare a few bars of soap?" Mother Teresa asked a shop owner nearby. "For the street children." The man shrugged and gave her a handful. Another man brought a table to the little outdoor school. Someone else sent a chair.

More and more children came running every time she opened her "school." She begged grocers for food and soon gave the hungry children something to eat at lunch. A local priest gave her a hundred rupees. When the class size swelled to sixty children every day, other volunteers came to teach them. Many people heard of the work the little nun was doing. They sent money, food, and supplies. Now some of the students learned sewing. They all learned how to behave together.

Mother Teresa opened a second outdoor school in another poor slum nearby. The children flocked there too. Next, she opened a dispensary, where medicines, food, and clothing were free for the poorest of the poor. She used a classroom at a nearby convent school. For supplies, she had to beg at businesses, shops, and churches. Mother Teresa hated begging, so she tried to remember that Jesus, on the Cross, had called out, "I thirst."

The slum children thirsted for learning, food, and love. Jesus had been thirsty for water but also for the love of his followers. *If Jesus could beg*, Mother Teresa thought, *I can beg*.

One morning she set out walking to look for a place to stay closer to Moti Jhil. By late afternoon, her legs ached. Her head did, too, and her feet were all blistered. "I know what the poor go through looking for shelter," she told the archbishop when he came to see how she was doing with her schools.

He had a surprise for her. "A friend of mine

will let you stay for free in the empty third floor of his house." Now all Mother Teresa needed for her Missionaries of Charity Order were ten new young nuns. There wasn't much time to find them. Her trial year was half over.

During the day, Mother Teresa worked at her schools and on the street. At night, she wrote letters to old students from the Entally Loreto. "Dear Subashini Das," she began. Subashini was a member of the girls' sodality that Mother Teresa began at the school. She wrote to all the sodality members and to other students as well.

A few days later, Subashini Das found Mother Teresa in her empty third-floor convent. "I want to join your order," she said. This first Missionary of Charity novice took the name Sister Agnes. Another of Mother Teresa's old students showed up a few days later. She became Sister Gertrude. All three women wore the same habit. Over a simple white dress, they wrapped a pure white *sari* pinned at the left shoulder with a small, dangling cross. Together they looked graceful and kind. Mother insisted that they look cheerful, too.

"I need these medicines," she said at a pharmacy one day. The pharmacist just laughed at her. Mother Teresa walked out to the sidewalk by his door, got down on her knees, and began praying. People walked around her or stepped over her. Some crossed the street to avoid her.

"Fine, then!" the pharmacist said, and stormed out of the building with a paper bag. "Here are your medicines. Now go away!" Mother Teresa and her nuns nursed anyone they found who was sick. First they cleaned wounds and sores. It was hard, sometimes, to get off all the dirt and pus and maggots.

"Pretend you are caring for Jesus," Mother Teresa told her nuns. "In a way, each victim *is* Jesus. Remember what it says in the Bible? 'As you do it for the least of these, my brothers . . .'"

"' . . . You do it for Me,'" Sister Gertrude

finished the quote. Mother Teresa held her out-stretched hand and repeated the end. With each word she folded one finger into Sister Gertrude's palm. Sister Gertrude smiled.

"That is *it*," Mother Teresa said. "Let the love of God shine through your face." Mother Teresa's radiant smiles brought more and more nuns to her little order. They all stayed in the third-floor room the archbishop had found for Mother Teresa. She put a crucifix on the wall and lettered a sign to go next to it: I THIRST.

The nuns slept side by side on the floor on mats. Mother Teresa kept a strict schedule by ringing a bell. They all attended Mass held by Father Henry at a nearby church. Mother Teresa kept everything tightly organized. The constitution she wrote for her order in 1949 left nothing to question. It added a fourth vow. Missionaries of Charity promised poverty, chastity, and obedience, like other orders did. They also had to vow to "give free and wholehearted service to the poor." On October 7, 1950, the archbishop issued his pronouncement: The Missionaries were now an official order in Calcutta.

In the next two years, twenty more novices joined the missionaries. Their days were all the same. The girls were awakened at 4:40 in the morning and prayed together at 5:00. They went to Mass at 5:45. After breakfast of tea and thin Indian bread came household chores and then work in the streets. They ate lunch at 12:30. Then they rested, read, or napped until 2:30. The nuns then began their serious worship, meditating or reading until 3:00. A light meal, tea, was served at 3:15, followed by prayers adoring God. Everyone went out again to the streets until 7:30. Prayers were at 9:00, and bed at 9:45.

And the order grew. Soon they needed more living space. More importantly, they needed a place to bring the poorest, sickest people they found on the streets. Three million people crowded into Calcutta. Hundreds died every day. The hospitals couldn't take all the sick.

The city didn't have the staff to handle them. So Mother Teresa struck a deal with Calcutta officials. They would give her abandoned property by the old temple of Kali if she would take care of the dying. "Kali?" Mother Teresa asked. "She is the Hindu goddess of creation and destruction, isn't she? Hindus would be happy to go there to die. Muslims and Christians wouldn't care—as long as they are cared for and loved."

Mother Teresa's heart soared as she toured the dirty, abandoned building. Rooms could be used as chapels and libraries, meeting rooms and offices. Hundreds of beds could fit downstairs. It had a kitchen. Bathrooms. Electricity. But it had filth, too.

The Missionaries of Charity quickly moved in. They brought buckets and soap, disinfectant and paintbrushes. Within days, the old building was open for business, renamed "the Place of the Pure Heart," or *Nirmal Hriday* in Bengali.

The first ward was for critically ill men who

had been found by the nuns or brought by the city. The second big room housed dying women. Everyone lay on plastic covered mats, with clean sheets and fresh pillows. As they passed away, their bodies were carefully carried to a hallway, where they lay under covers until the city collected them.

The Sisters of Charity allowed visitors any-time. At first glance, the Nirmal Hriday looked like a horror house. Every bed held a very sick body. Some moaned. Others thrashed and cursed. Most were hard to look at. Some were in comas. A few were dead.

"I don't know where to start!" one young Bengali nun said. "There are just too many!"

"Just love them," Mother Teresa said, "one by one." In the Bengali language, "one by one" sounded like *"Ek, ek, ek."* She had to laugh. And the new sister laughed along.

As visitors watched, the sisters moved quietly bed to bed. They held hands with frightened patients. "You are not alone," they said, wiping a fevered forehead with cool cloths. "I love you. I am here for you." They prayed with those who wished it. For others they had cool water to drink, candy, or a last cigarette. Every wound was gently cleaned and bandaged. Every head was shampooed and lovingly towel-dried. One by one, a visitor could see little miracles as victims relaxed and died in peace.

The city health authorities did not allow lepers to be brought to Nirml Hriday. Leprosy, a dreadful, slow disease, kills nerves. Without medicine, a leper's numb fingers and toes, nose, and ears are often battered bloody or broken off. The victims do not feel it when it happens. They don't feel the pain of the sores and infections that follow. A huge city like Calcutta had thousands of lepers too poor to get medicine and good care.

Mother Teresa found a house and the medicine the lepers needed. She found them the way she managed everything about the Sisters of Charity: She begged. She described what God was doing through her order. She told stories about the people she had saved—and those who had died with her in peace.

"I have a great gift just for you," she often told people. That got their interest. Then she would say, "It is a special way for you to do something wonderful for God." Then she described what the Sisters of Charity needed. It could be money, food, medicine, housing, or a job that needed doing. Sometimes people said no. More often they said yes, charmed by little Mother's smile and inspired by her faith.

Besides the leper's hospital, Nirmal Hriday, and the slum schools, Mother Teresa founded an orphanage in 1953. The nuns cared for hundreds of abandoned babies there. Like all of her missionaries, Mother Teresa slept on a thin mat on the floor. She had only two *saris*, one to wear, one to wash. Both of her *saris*, like those of all professed nuns, had blue stripes running the length of the edges. Novices' *saris* had no stripes. One bucket was assigned to Mother Teresa, where she could wash a *sari* before hanging it up to dry. Her food was simple, cooked on a charcoal fire.

But she lived in bliss. She was using all her talents of leadership and management, she was teaching, and she was following Jesus' words, delivered directly to her. What more could she want?

CHAPTER EIGHT
THE WORLD CALLS

Nearly one hundred sisters lived in the mother house in Calcutta in 1960—and the order was barely ten years old. Calcutta officials trusted Mother Teresa now. She spoke simply and honestly to everyone about her faith. "Give only all to God," she told people. It sounded strange at first, but it stuck in their minds.

She raised money wherever she thought she could get it. She created new schools in other slum neighborhoods. Now they had books as well as soap, paper, and pencils instead of sticks and dirt. Her orphanage had cribs, instead of mats on the floor. Mother Teresa provided milk for the poor, delivered medicine for lepers, and arranged to have wells drilled for clean water. She coordinated helpful volunteers. Still, her most important tool was love.

As a mother superior of her order, she had endless details to handle. She made it seem easy. Though she only slept an hour or two most nights, Mother Teresa seemed tireless.

"Go and live with the poorest of the poor." Jesus' words echoed in her mind. She was doing His wishes. Whenever she felt overwhelmed, or exhausted, or insecure, she remembered the tone of His voice. She pictured his face. After all, He had asked her personally to take this all on. He would provide whatever she needed. All she had to do was ask.

"There are desperate poor in cities all over India," she said to Father Henry. "Can we do nothing for them?" He knew what she wanted. He wrote letters to her superiors and to the new pope in Rome, Italy. Pope John Paul XXIII already knew about Mother Teresa. He'd read about her in church magazines and had spoken to people who'd seen her at work in the slums. He liked the way she made the poor feel closer to God. The pope agreed that she could start opening new convents of the Missionaries of Charity thoughout India.

Pope John Paul XXIII was busy. He held a huge meeting at the Vatican, the Church's center, in Rome. Three thousand bishops, archbishops, and cardinals came. So did Roman Catholic professors and leaders from all over the world. The pope wanted these faithful men to pray together at the Vatican Council. He expected God to speak through these men, giving them new ideas. His dear church had not changed much in centuries. But all around it, people had changed.

They had just been through two world wars. They had seen the evil of Nazism and the amazing sight of a man on the moon. Telephones and radios put them in touch with others everywhere. It seemed that television had become a center of family life, not prayer. The people needed to feel closer to God. The Church needed new ways to pull

Roman Catholics together. And it needed spiritual vitality to match the times. The Church was ready, the pope thought, to lead the world to peace.

Mother Teresa worked on a smaller scale than the pope, one poor person at a time. "The Little Flower is a most wonderful example," she told people, speaking of Saint Therese of Lisieux. "She did small things with great love. Ordinary things with extraordinary love. That is why she became a great saint."

Mother Teresa always made time in her day for those small things. She held a lonely little baby until he stopped crying. She carefully wiped a leper's sores and covered them with clean bandages. She talked with a dying man about heaven. In all of their faces, she saw the face of Jesus. More women joined in her work. Men, too, wondered if they might help by becoming Brother Missionaries of Charity. Mother Teresa's love seemed to bring out the best in everyone.

She even seemed to charm animals. One day she stepped outside to see what was making people scream. A bull, frightened and confused, galloped down the street. Stalls selling vegetables and gems, cloth and spicy food blocked his way. He was angry—and dangerous. Mother Teresa stepped quietly into his path. She held out her hand and waited. The bull screeched to a halt and snorted. He stared at her calm face. Then he stepped forward and gently sniffed her tiny hand.

People reacted to her holiness, too. Once they had met her, they volunteered to help. Or they offered supplies and food to "her" mission. Or they asked how they, too, could become missionaries of charity. The effect lasted long after meeting the little nun.

In the 1960s, a small group of her followers left to open new branches of the Missionaries of Charity in one city after another in India. Mother Teresa knew that her nuns, her "little seedlings would need frequent watering and care." But how would she visit them? Traveling across such a huge country was expensive. Mother Teresa wanted all the money collected for her order to go to the poor. What was she to do?

Jawaharlal Nehru, the president of the newly independent India, gave her a free pass on Air India so she could fly anywhere in the country, anytime in the service of the poor.

There were desperately poor people outside of India too. Mother Teresa got letters from cities everywhere, begging her to bring her sisters to help in their country. In July of 1965, Mother Teresa was given permission to expand into other countries. Missionaries of Charity convent opened in the slums of Cocorote, Venezuela. Within a few years her order was helping the poor right outside the Vatican, in Rome, Italy, and in London, Australia, Africa, and even the Bronx, in New York City.

Pope John Paul XXIII died before all of his meetings were finished. A new pope, Paul VI, was elected by the cardinals to take his place.

With permission from Pope Paul VI, Mother Teresa helped organize an order of brothers to do the same work as her sisters.

She organized a worldwide network of spiritual supporters, too. These "coworkers" were all in pain from some disease. That was a requirement. Most coworkers were unable to work or live normally. Mother Teresa gave them a job: They were to smile because God loved them so dearly that he was showing them exactly how Jesus suffered on the Cross. She said, "Suffering—pain, humiliation, sickness, and failure—is but a kiss of Jesus." The coworkers were to pray constantly for Jesus to help the work of the missionaries. This gave their lives a focus. The successes of Mother Teresa's movement became their success. And all the prayers to God seemed to be working.

A new group of women began vowing to help. Instead of going out into the community, these new nuns would spend their entire lives in prayer, cloistered in a convent. The force of the Contemplative Missionaries of Charity's prayers, Mother Teresa knew, would have enormous effects on people.

It did. A new order of men formed, cloistered like the new sisters. The prayers and adoration from all these Contemplative monks would bring even more of God's strength to the Missionaries of Charity—and help to the poor, worldwide. Mother Teresa kept everyone working together while the Missionaries of Charity made all these big changes.

The Roman Catholic Church's rules hadn't been changed in well over a thousand years. It was due for some adjustments, too. Before he died, Pope John Paul XXIII had called a second Vatican Council to come up with new, more modern rules for the Church. He was old and sick. He knew he was going to die, but he wanted to leave his church ready to thrive in a modern world.

Like Mother Teresa, most people had grown up under the old rules. Even little changes were uncomfortable. But Vatican II made big changes, starting with language. Mother Teresa had loved knowing that everywhere in the world, Mass was said with precisely the same Latin words. Two thousand years ago, everyone understood Latin. Now, hardly anyone did. So Pope Paul XXIII announced that the priests had to speak in the language of their church members.

So that people would feel they were a welcome part of the Mass, priests turned to face them instead of speaking toward the wall behind the altar. Priests could hand the blessed Sacrament to people—and then they could feed themselves. No priest would ever embarrass anyone by slapping them again during Confirmation. And the "altar rail" was removed from churches. It looked too much like a fence keeping people out.

Now, church members—men and *women*—were allowed to read the Bible during Mass. They were encouraged to read the Bible on their own, too. Even in the convents, nuns could think for themselves about what the Bible meant.

Pope John Paul XXIII began building bridges to other faiths too. Suddenly, the Church meant Roman Catholics *and* Eastern Catholics. Anyone who worshipped Jesus was a "Christian." Church members and priests banded together with other churches, synagogues, and temples. They worked on social causes, like peace, justice, ecology, racism, and poverty. A new sense of activism swept the Church.

Mother Teresa had been active all along.

Letters came to her from around the world, asking, "What can we do to help?" These people weren't sick enough to be coworkers. They couldn't join her religious orders either. Perhaps they were married. Or they had parents they had to care for. They just couldn't promise to spend the rest of their lives in poverty, chastity, obedience, and service to the poor. Many of them weren't even Roman Catholics. But they had all been inspired by

Mother Teresa's example. They offered their help.

Mother Teresa knew they'd all been sent by God. Working with others, Mother Teresa set up a huge mailing list, welcoming these new people into her community. She asked them to raise funds, to donate supplies, to go to the slums and help out, and—of course—to pray.

"The fruit of prayer is a deepening faith," she told them. "And the fruit of faith is love. And the fruit of love is service."

A world of good—of people helping others— spread outward from this one little woman.

"I do this," she told everyone, "because I believe I am doing it for Jesus. I am very sure that this is His work. It comes from Jesus. Not from me. I am very sure."

CHAPTER NINE
SUFFERING IN SILENCE

Not everyone was impressed when they saw Mother Teresa's overwhelming accomplishments on TV.

"It is easy for her. She's a nun," people said. "She doesn't have any kids to raise. She doesn't have a job. She doesn't have doubts like the rest of us."

It was true that Mother Teresa smiled all the time. She told all of her nuns to smile too. "Let God shine through for others to see," she told them. It didn't matter if they were tired or sore, hungry or discouraged. "Smile," she would say firmly. And she smiled to show them how.

But Mother Teresa's smile covered real agony. From the very beginning of her work alone on the streets, Mother Teresa was full of doubt.

Jesus had actually spoken with her on the train, that much seemed clear to her. Then she had obediently followed His directions to Calcutta, but it had not been easy.

Things were bad when she got there. She was terribly lonely after the constant companionship of women in the convents. She was dirty most of the time. The roads always seemed to be ankle deep in red dust or deeper in monsoon puddles filled with trash, waste, and mud. Some people made fun of the white woman in a *sari*. A few even threw rocks at her.

Wherever she looked there was more work than she ever could do. There were so many poor to help! It looked hopeless. *Ek, Ek, Ek,* Mother Teresa told herself. *One by one.* Then she smiled so she would not cry.

If only Jesus would talk to me again, she thought. He had done it once, on the train. Mother Teresa really needed to hear that she was doing things right. She needed to hear He was pleased. She just needed the sound of His voice.

She caught glimpses of Him in the first year. She heard echoes of His voice. But after a while, it was just silence. There had been no word from Him for many years.

When the first little children had gathered at Moti Jhil, Mother Teresa told herself they were a sign from God. She felt bursts of joy when one of the boys said "please," when one of the little ones reached for soap to wash himself, and when one girl called her "Ma." Perhaps, she thought, joy was how Jesus would communicate with her now.

But why didn't he *speak*?

When six long months had passed in her first year in Calcutta and she still had no nuns for her new order, Mother Teresa doubted everything. She confessed her lack of faith to the priest. "Pray with me," the calm voice said from behind the slatted window.

In prayer, Mother Teresa grew calm. As always, the Rosary was a comfort. So were the bursts of joy her work began to bring to her. Followers arrived. Gifts came without warning:

housing, medicine, blankets, and bedpans. A second school. A third.

Mother Teresa took those gifts as messages that she was doing the right things. So she did more. And more.

Every time she glanced at the crucifix on the wall, she read the sign she'd put beside it: I THIRST. The words hung in chapel, every bedroom, every sickroom, and every school.

"He is thirsty for *you*," Mother Teresa told her nuns. She sent it in letters to distant convents. She told the brothers and the coworkers, too. "Jesus loves you, but even more, he ardently desires you. He misses you when you do not come close to him. He loves you always even when you do not feel worthy of him. When you are not accepted by others—even sometimes by yourself—He always accepts you."

Mother Teresa brought many souls to God. Sometimes she baptized the dying people she found on the streets—but only if they said they didn't mind. She baptized the orphan babies who were rescued. Mother kept holy water ready at the orphanage and at the house for the dying. First she said the person's name, then, "I baptize you in the name of the Father." A little water was poured on the head. "And of the Son." More water. "And of the Holy Ghost." A third wetting. She and her nuns were always ready to do this, bonding another person into the Roman Catholic community.

This gave her great joy. She knew she was doing God's work through the church. Jesus thirsted for souls, and she could bring them to Him. The local Muslims and Hindus might not be so willing to have her in Calcutta if they thought she was stealing their souls for the Catholic Church. That's why she and her nuns always asked before they baptized. And she always remembered what the nursing nuns had said: "Take care of their bodies first."

As her order grew, she did everything she thought Jesus wanted of her. She prayed constantly, year after year. And yet she did not hear His blessed voice again.

She had to tell herself it really *did* happen.

She had to go on faith that she was not wasting her life—and the lives of all of her followers. And she kept smiling for everyone to see.

Sometimes when she was very tired, or when another war began in the world, or when one of her precious nuns quit, she lost faith. Mother Teresa wondered if He had really spoken to her. Could she have imagined it? In her darkest moments she even wondered if *He* existed. How could any God allow so much suffering in the world?

She told her priest about these terrifying doubts.

"Perhaps this is a test," he said in a darkened confession booth. "Perhaps God is leaving you alone to see if you will keep doing good without His presence."

"But I am so very lonely." Mother Teresa heard the catch in her voice as tears threatened. "Did I do something wrong, Father? Will He ever come back?" She heard the priest shift closer on the other side of the window.

"You are not alone," the priest said. "Remember being slapped when you were confirmed? That was a warning that things would be tough sometimes. Several of the saints, the priests, and church teachers have gone through a testing like yours. God lets them feel abandoned for a while. He lets them really suffer. This test even has a name. It is called "the dark night of the soul.""

Mother Teresa sat silent for a moment in the dark booth. That was just how it felt. After feeling completely safe in her faith, this "test" was terrifying. She felt as if she were out alone and lost on a dark and stormy night. Perhaps she was out in the ocean. She felt in real danger of drowning. And she didn't know anymore if there would be a heaven waiting for her.

"How long does this 'dark night' last?" she asked. Mother Teresa was almost afraid to ask.

"For some people," the priest said gently, "for the ones he loves most, God's testing can last a very long time."

Mother Teresa left the booth, scared to her

core. But now when the doubts tore at her faith, she could think of it as a test. Others had passed it. They kept on believing there was a God. They kept living according to his will.

It is almost like being tortured, she thought. *But I won't give in.*

Through the ages, Christians had been burned at the stake or twisted to death on racks. They had been dunked in water or shot full of arrows. Their captors were trying to force them to say, "There is no God," or, "Jesus is a lie," or even, "The Church is evil." The real saints died without ever giving up. They kept their faith to the end. Those martyrs were true church heroes.

Mother Teresa put a joyous smile on her face. She knew what she had to do. She straightened her *sari* and went out again to serve the poorest of the poor.

CHAPTER TEN
SUCCESS

"I can't go to get this award," Mother Teresa grumbled. "I am needed right here."

In 1962, new Missionaries of Charity convents were opening all over the world. The novice nuns needed her encouragement. She needed to find someone to donate more money so they could buy a well, open a clinic, start a school. The needs were endless.

"Go, Mother," her friends said. "The Indian government is right. You deserve their highest honor, the Order of the Lotus, for the work you have done." Mother did not give in until someone pointed out, "Many people will see the ceremony. Others will read of it. They will have to think of the poor. And perhaps they will send us donations?"

"Fine, then," Mother Teresa said. "I will go. But I won't waste our money on fancy clothes. This old *sari* is good enough for the poor. It is good enough for the rich and famous to see."

While she was away from her convents, Mother Teresa took a plane to Rome to meet her brother, Lazar. He was terribly upset. Albania's new government was harsh and cruel. It had closed its borders and would not let anybody in or out. "Mama is old and frail," Lazar said. "Agatha is there with her, but I don't know how safe they are."

Mother Teresa flew home knowing she would try to get her mother out of Albania. If she didn't, she might never see her again.

When she got back from the awards ceremony, she gave all her prize money to the order of the Missionaries of Charity. Then she went right back to work.

Her friends were right. Donations arrived from all over India. Mother Teresa would not let the nuns use it to buy fans or air conditioners for the convents. They could not get regular beds with sheets and pillows to sleep in. "No washing machines, either," Mother Teresa said as nuns filed by silently. Each woman carried her bucket full of soapy water and a dirty sari. "If the poorest of the poor don't have it, we won't have it either. Remember your vows."

That same year she received the Magsaysay Prize. The head of the Conference of Asiatic States made her come up on stage. "This award," he said, "is given every year to the most worthy woman in Asia."

This time, Mother Teresa took advantage of the stage. She smiled at the audience and all the cameras. Then she said, "I accept this prize in the name of the thousands and thousands of poor people living in your slums."

It was not what people expected to hear. Mother Teresa went on: "While we sit here over a fancy dinner, they die of hunger. While we celebrate with our families, they die alone and homeless. Worst of all, they die unloved. They need your help. It is in their name that I thank you."

When she left the stage there was a long, stunned silence. Applause began slowly. It swelled until the entire room was standing.

As she flew home from the event, Mother Teresa thought of how she could have made her speech better. Maybe she should start with a happy story of a child in one of her orphanages. That would make people feel good. Then she could tell a horror story about what it is like to die in the streets. *That* would get people's attention! She could talk more about Jesus, and His love. She could quote the Bible. And then she could make her pitch for help.

As she grew more famous and her speeches got better, churches and schools asked her to come and speak. It took her away from work with the poor, but it did bring in money for her order. She always sent some of her income to the Vatican for the Church to use too. Mother Teresa enjoyed giving speeches. It was like teaching on a very big scale. Jesus would be pleased, she hoped. She still had no clear sign from Him, but she went on in stubborn faith.

She never gave up on getting her mother
and sister out of Albania either. She had written letters and spoken to officials. She had
applied for the forms they needed—but nothing ever came of it. In 1972, Mama Bojaxhiu
died. Within two years, Agatha was dead too.
The last time Mother Teresa had seen either of
them was fifty years earlier, waving at her
through a moving train window.

In the 1970s she received many awards. She
flew to the United States for a Kennedy
Foundation award. She got the Good Sama-
ritan prize too. At the Vatican, the pope gave
her the Pope John XXIII Peace Prize. She flew
to London, England, Paris, France, and San
Francisco, California, to receive more awards.
While she was in these countries, she stopped
at Missionaries of Charity convents there.
She encouraged the nuns and brothers. She
thanked the coworkers and volunteers. And
she always took the time to cradle abandoned
babies. Famous as she had become, she always
stopped at the missions. "God loves you," she

said, wiping the face of a sick man. "Do not be afraid," she crooned, holding a cup while a dying woman sipped water. "You are going to a beautiful place."

Her speeches began to sound more like sermons. "At the end of our life," she would say, "we will not be judged by how many diplomas we have received, by how much money we have made, or how many great things we have done." Mother Teresa would let the silence stretch a moment. Then she would say, "We all will be judged by how we treat Christ in his most distressing disguise."

Mother Teresa was nearing seventy years old now, and showing it. Her body was shrunken; her posture, bent. Her hands were knobby with arthritis. Her face was a maze of wrinkles. Day after day, she rose at 5:30 in the morning. She still kept herself to the full-time schedule of prayer and service of her order.

In 1979, she traveled to Oslo, Norway, to receive one of the greatest awards in the world. "Mother Teresa wins the Nobel Peace Prize!"

the headlines screamed. Her face smiled from the cover of *Time* magazine and *Newsweek*, too. People began calling her "a living saint."

At the Nobel Peace Prize ceremony, Mother Teresa stood in her old $1.90 *sari* in front of a room filled with royalty from around the world. "There is no dinner for you tonight," she told the elegant guests. "I have asked that the cost of this one meal, three thousand dollars, be sent to my mission. That will pay for an entire year's food for four hundred children in Calcutta." She showed the ultra-rich guests just how unfair it was that they lived in such splendor while the poor suffered such poverty. Then she told them how she dealt with this seemingly hopeless situation.

"I never look at the masses as my responsibility," she said. "I look at the individual. I can love only one person at a time. I can feed only one person at a time. Just one by one."

She did not take a break after receiving the Nobel Peace Prize. She went right back to her work around the world. Now when she talked, she spoke more often about the lack of love in the world than the lack of money. "People are hungry not only for bread today, but for love," she explained. "They are naked not just because they lack clothes. They lack human dignity and respect. They are homeless because their loved ones have rejected them."

Mother Teresa got to see her beloved brother once more in Rome. A long-time smoker, he was suffering from lung cancer. When she flew away, she knew he was dying. In 1981, she got the word that he had passed away.

Sometimes her speeches wandered a bit now as her tired mind fought to keep her body going for Jesus' work. She now always remembered to say something against abortion. She preached on how important families were—and love.

The next year and again in 1983 she had to be hospitalized with heart pains. "I have to get out," she told the doctors. "My poor need me," she complained to the nurses. "Why are you wasting your time with me? I don't need all this food . . . all these clean sheets . . . all this medicine. There are millions of poor people out there who need them more than I do!"

When she was discharged, the doctors wrote on her chart that she was "a very difficult patient."

They also told her she would have to cut down on her travels.

But the honors kept coming. The United Nations awarded her with their Nobel Peace Prize in 1979. In 1985, Ronald Reagan gave her the Presidential Medal of Freedom. She was made an honorary United States citizen in 1996. The Knights of Columbus, an important Roman Catholic men's club, gave her a prize too. They thanked her for "outstanding contributions to the Catholic Church and society."

She was still waiting to hear from Jesus. Her soul's horrible "dark night" had lasted fifty years. Her faith had been tested for a lifetime, but now she did not falter. She could look around at the good she had done and know it had to please God.

At eighty years old, she still cleaned wounds

and fed babies. She received Mass every morning and said the Rosary every evening. Everyone in the world knew about her. The tiny woman's life of service and faith inspired people to live better lives. Whenever she was sick now, the world held its breath. Newspaper headlines followed her decline.

Instead of sleep, her nights were filled with nightmares. Terrors swept over her, and she awoke screaming. Sometimes she had barely fallen asleep when she began to shriek. She called out for Jesus, of course. He did not answer. She kept the other nuns awake in the convents with her horrors. Admitted to the hospital in Calcutta in 1996 for chest pains, she yelled and thrashed in the hospital bed, fighting in the dark night.

The doctors could do nothing. This was a struggle going on within her mind and soul, not her body. If she did not get rest, the doctors told her priest, she would not survive. The priest spoke with his superior. Some terrible problem was eating away at Mother Teresa. Prayer would not budge it. Confession did not lighten her load. Her problem had taken possession of her. There was one special ceremony that the church held in reserve for cases like this.

They asked Mother Teresa if she would like them to try an exorcism to cast out whatever evil thoughts were taking over her mind at night. She was ready to try anything.

First the priest made sure there was a crucifix present in her room. He made the sign of the cross and sprinkled holy water around the bed and on Mother Teresa. Then he read a list of the saints and prayed for God's help. He read psalms from the Bible, and parts of Jesus' story, too. He laid his hands on Mother Teresa, and they recited the Catholic Creed, the baptismal ceremony, and the Our Father.

Then the priest held up his own cross and traced the sign of the cross on his own forehead. "I order you, Satan. . . ." He spoke directly to the negative force that had taken control of Mother Teresa's mind. He used the exact words that had been spoken since 1614, when they were first written down. Sometimes it worked. Sometimes it didn't.

". . . Therefore, go back, Satan." It was done. The priest chanted a thanksgiving, prayed again, and blessed the old nun.

Mother Teresa left the hospital a few days later. The doctors had implanted a pacemaker. She slept better, and no one else was awakened by her wild screams. After confession, Mother Teresa always felt light. The guilt was gone. After the exorcism, she felt right. She could relax again. The worries and memories she could no longer control were gone. It was time to get back to work.

Mother Teresa was tired. She still gave occasional speeches. She helped by holding babies in the nursery. She interviewed new postulants, but now she asked to resign from her duties as Superior General. Her Mother Superiors prayed about it. They met. They prayed some more. And they said, "No. We need you here. The poor need you."

Mother Teresa had taken a vow of obedience. She agreed to stay on in the job without complaint. But her health was failing. She suffered from bouts of malaria. Her heart gave her pains. She fell and broke ribs. She spent more time in hospitals. Finally, in March of 1997, the order named a new Mother Superior.

"But don't you call me 'Mother,'" Sister Nirmala said as she was introduced. "There is only one Mother in this order—and she still lives." But everyone knew she couldn't last much longer.

On Friday, September 5, 1997, Mother Teresa lay dying at the mother house in Calcutta. She was not afraid. Soon, she was sure, she would be talking with Jesus again at last. A crowd of her nuns gathered around, their *saris* making them look like angels. The priest gave her last rites and heard her last confession. The nuns began to sing quietly. Then, with a smile on her face, Mother Teresa slipped out of this life and into the next.

CHAPTER ELEVEN
SAINTHOOD?

The news of Mother Teresa's death flashed through radios and televisions everywhere. Everybody knew of "the Saint of the Gutters." They thought they knew how special she was. Now information about all her accomplishments startled everyone.

At the time of her death, Mother Teresa's Missionaries of Charity had over four thousand sisters. There were three hundred brothers and over one hundred *thousand* volunteers. They lived and worked in 123 countries in 610 missions. That one little woman from Skopje had been responsible for starting the entire organization—and for all the good it did around the world.

They had homes for people with HIV/AIDS,

leprosy, and tuberculosis. Missionaries ran soup kitchens, orphanages, homes for the dying, schools, and counseling programs.

Mother Teresa's funeral began in the slums. From the mother house where her nuns said their good-byes, she was driven in a Missionaries of Charity ambulance that simply said MOTHER across the front. The poorest of the poor paid their last respects to her as she lay in a free day school. She was picked up in the wagon that had carried the bodies of Mahatma Gandhi, and then Jawaharlal Nehru. It drove her through the streets of Calcutta, where hundreds of thousands of Indians stood in silent respect. A final Mass as said in a covered sports stadium filled with heads of state, movie stars, and dignitaries from around the world. She was buried beneath a plain stone slab in the mother house.

Famous people everywhere spoke of how wonderful she was. The United Nations Secretary-General said, "She IS the United Nations. She is peace in the World."

The president of Pakistan called her "rare" and said she was "one of the highest examples of service to humanity."

She was called "the twentieth century's most famous woman."

Pope John Paul II wanted to make her an official saint of the Catholic Church. She was the holiest woman he had ever known. She inspired people who belonged to the Church and those who did not. They loved her, and so did he.

There was one problem. The path to sainthood is long and slow. It isn't even supposed to start until a person has been dead for five years.

People were already carrying medals of Mother Teresa as if she were truly a saint. They had photos and statues of her in their homes. John Paul II put her on a "fast track" to sainthood by forgiving the five-year waiting period.

He appointed a priest to research her life, looking for evidence for—and against—her sainthood. Then he had to wait for a miracle.

Somewhere, some time, a cure or a miraculous event had to happen before the next step in making Mother Teresa a saint.

Monica Besra, a cancer patient in India, was in terrible pain from a tumor in her belly. She'd been to the hospital. She'd done whatever the doctors decided, but nothing seemed to be working. All she could think about was what would happen to her young children if she died. Suddenly the cramps became unbearable. Monica took off the locket she wore and rubbed her belly with it. She reported that a strange light seemed to flood outward from the picture in the locket—a picture of Mother Teresa. At that same moment, her pain began to ease. Within hours, the tumor shrank away to nothing.

That was the miracle John Paul II needed. After it was investigated for truth, the Vatican accepted it. It was evidence of her powers even beyond death. John Paul II elevated Mother Teresa to "Blessed Teresa of Calcutta." He chose September 5 as her official day. Then he settled down to wait for a second miracle to be reported and investigated. After that, Blessed Teresa could become Saint Teresa. John Paul II died before it all happened. Now the new pope, Benedict XVI, will be watching.

Meanwhile, Blessed Teresa's work goes on. Young women and men join her orders every year. They experience the Missionaries of Charity as postulants for a year, then they become novices. Finally, if they are very sure, they take the four vows, poverty, chastity, obedience, and service to the poor.

As you read this, young nuns in white *saris* are wandering the world's worst slums, two by two. Strong, young monks in white pants and tunics search for the poorest of the poor. When they find a stranger in pain, who is lost, alone, and hungry, they don't stop to think about it. They don't talk it over. They drop everything and help. They own nothing but love.

More than three thousand other volunteers show up in Calcutta every year, asking what they can do to help. Around the world these volunteers help the poorest of the poor, one by one. Others simply keep Blessed Teresa statues to inspire them to be gentler, kinder, more loving. Perhaps they carry her medal in a pocket or on a chain. They put her special day, September 5, on their calendar. They remember her words, and they smile.

> *The more you smile at God,*
> *the more you smile at others,*
> *the more you smile at yourself,*
> *the holier you become.*

—BLESSED MOTHER TERESA OF CALCUTTA

MOTHER TERESA
TIME LINE

1910: Agnes Gonxha Bojaxhiu is born on August 26, in Skopje, in what is now Macedonia

1928: Becomes Sister Teresa of the Child Jesus, novitiate in Loreto order

1929: Arrives in Calcutta to teach at Loreto Entally

1937: Takes final vows, becoming Mother Teresa of the Child Jesus

1946: Received a calling from Jesus "to serve him among the poorest of the poor"

1947: Moves to Calcutta's slums to set up her first school

1950: Founds the order of the Missionaries of Charity; becomes citizen of India

1952: Opens Nirmal Hriday, or "Pure Heart," a home for the dying

1979: Accepts Nobel Peace Prize on behalf of the poor

1997: Steps down on March 13 as head of her order

1997: Dies on September 5, in Calcutta, India

2002: The first of three miracles required for canonization as a saint—the curing of a cancer—accepted by Pope John Paul II

2003: Becomes "Blessed Teresa of Calcutta" when beatified by Pope John Paul II

FOR FURTHER READING

PICTURE BOOKS

Demi. *Mother Teresa*. New York: Margaret K. McElderry Books, 2005.

Schafer, Lola M. *Mother Teresa. First Biographies series*. New York: Capstone Press, 2003.

MIDDLE GRADE BOOKS

Wellman, Sam. *Mother Teresa: Missionary of Charity*. Philadelphia: Chelsea House, 1999.

MOTHER TERESA'S WRITINGS

Teresa, Mother. *Words to Love by . . .* Notre Dame, IN: Ave Maria Press, 1983.

———. *Mother Teresa: In My Own Words*. Liguori, MO: Liguori Press, 1996.

FOR ADULTS

Sebba, Anne. *Mother Teresa: Beyond the Image*. New York: Doubleday, 1997.

Spink, Katherine. *Mother Teresa: A Complete, Authorized Biography*. New York: HarperCollins, 1997.

Vazhakala, Fr. Sebastian, MC. *My Life with Mother Teresa: My Thirty-Year Friendship with the Mother of the Poor*. Cincinnati: St. Anthony Messenger Press, 2004.

VIDEO

Arts & Entertainment Biography Series. *Mother Teresa: A Life of Devotion*.

AUDIO

Tartaglia, Dr. Lou, and Father Angelo Scolozzi. *Thirsting For God: The Spiritual Lessons of Mother Teresa*. New York: Simon & Schuster Audio.

INTERNET

Mother Teresa of Calcutta, Official site of the Cause for Canonization:
www.motherteresacause.info

Mother Teresa of Calcutta, Peacemaker, Pioneer, Legend:
www.ewtn.com/motherteresa

CHILDHOOD OF WORLD FIGURES

CHRISTOPHER COLUMBUS

ANNE FRANK

DIANA, PRINCESS OF WALES

POPE JOHN PAUL II

LEONARDO DA VINCI

MOTHER TERESA

COMING SOON:

GANDHI

★ ★ COLLECT THEM ALL! ★ ★